The People's History

Cullercoats

Not Just A Village, A Unique Place To Live

by Ron Wright

Cullercoats Bay, 2002, looking south.

Previous page: Cullercoats Bay, 1835, before the popular use of photography.

First published in 2002 by

The People's History Ltd
Suite 1
Byron House
Seaham Grange Business Park
Seaham
Co. Durham
SR7 0PY

ISBN 1 902527 63 1

Contents

Thank you for buying this book, *Cullercoats*.
To see the latest range of books available in The People's History series, and a
selection of historical prints we have on offer, please visit our website:

www.thepeopleshistory.co.uk

This is believed to be one of the first known photographs of Cullercoats Bay, *circa* 1850. The three storey building on the far left is the Ship Inn, which was demolished, to make way for the Hudleston Arms now renamed the Bay Hotel.

Dial House with the Queens Head public house behind it. The Queens Head survives today well into its second century as an inn.

Introduction

The village of Cullercoats sits high on the cliffs overlooking the North Sea about two miles north of Tynemouth and one mile south of Whitley Bay. Both of these adjacent towns have pressed ever closer inwards to Cullercoats, yet despite this encroachment, Cullercoats remains a clearly defined and singular place that retains its own identity.

An aerial view of Cullercoats Bay as it was in 1928 and as it should have been kept when the village was redeveloped.

Cullercoats has always felt as if it was being pushed into the cold grey North Sea, clinging as it does to the cliff tops like a barnacle on the hull of a ship. The planners and redevelopers of the 1960s may have tried to rob the village of its heritage, its quaint fishermen's cottages, narrow streets and alleyways but the village and the people living in it have preserved a record of its way of life. Many of the original families still live within the boundaries of Cullercoats and they still zealously guard and uphold many of the traditions which made this small village so famous for almost a century.

Little now remains of the fishing industry, the fishermen and the fishwives who hawked the daily catch far and wide, but fortunately much of the village's rich history was documented and recorded for posterity.

This book seeks to give the reader an insight into a unique village, its customs and personalities. It is not intended that every facet of history is covered and in some instances certain occurrences, even when they are in the public domain, have been deliberately omitted to save embarrassment to surviving relatives.

Acknowledgements

Following the publication of my first book *Beyond The Piers* it seemed a natural progression to write a book about the history of Cullercoats where I have lived for almost thirty years amongst its rich history. I have been in love with Cullercoats since my early childhood when my 'Nana Pop' brought me down from Newcastle on the red electric train.

'Nana Pop' was my grandmother from my father's side and was called Nora Wright. She lived in Snow Street, Newcastle and was christened 'Nana Pop' by myself when I could first talk. I used to run down the Victorian street with its cobbled road towards her door shouting 'Nana – pop' knowing that she always kept bottles of Tizer and lemonade in the larder. From that day onwards she was always referred to as 'Nana Pop.'

'Nana Pop' used to look after me on a Saturday and we frequently came down to the coast. We never visited Whitley Bay or Tynemouth, always Cullercoats. My 'Nana Pop' loved her fish and chips and we would always indulge ourselves whilst sitting on the beach amongst the fishermen's cobles. There is no finer dish especially when it is washed down with a bottle of Tizer with a little sand thrown in.

The preparation of this book would have taken much longer had it not been for the unselfish and unstinting help of Peter Burns who I regard as an obsessive researcher. His collection of newspaper cuttings, photographs, memorabilia and personal memories of Cullercoats has been of great assistance.

This book is dedicated to Peter as a mark of my respect for him and to my long ago departed 'Nana Pop' for introducing me to Cullercoats in my formative years.

I must also pay tribute to the following people who have kindly donated press cuttings, photographs and personal stories: Joan Patterson, Doreen and Frank Goodfellow, Susan Johnson, Tony Harrison, Rosalind Bailey, Steve Shannon, Joan Philips, Trish McGlasson, Charlie Steel and to the services offered and assistance received from Chris Lambert of Tynemouth Volunteer Life Brigade, Robert Oliver of the RNLI Station at Cullercoats, North Shields Library, Newcastle City Library, Tyne and Wear Archives and the Northumberland Public Records Office.

THE ORIGIN OF CULLERCOATS

Bell Storey's shop in Back Row, Cullercoats, now just a distant memory.

Despite its abundance of history the little village of Cullercoats is only just over three hundred years old. In comparative terms to its surroundings it is a mere youngster yet the village is known throughout the world, which makes it even more remarkable.

The name Cullercoats is a corruption of a number of previous names used for the hamlet and later village and was initially recorded as *Culfre-cots*. Culfer is the Anglo-Saxon name for dove and cots is plural for house and the name in translation means Dove Cote or Dove House.

The monks of Tynemouth Priory originally owned the land where Cullercoats stands and Marden Mill stood at the foot of Marden Burn in 1295 when it was one of six mills owned by Tynemouth Priory. The monks of Tynemouth kept pigeons for table food and it is possible that the first name used originated from this connection. Marden Burn is no longer visible but it can be traced running up a depression at the side of Eskdale Terrace. The mill is believed to have stood on the site currently occupied by the Fishermen's Mission.

It is believed that in 1315 coal was worked from drift mines in the area but this industry was destroyed by the Scottish invasions.

In 1483 Richard III gave £100 to Prior Boston of Tynemouth Priory for the maintenance of Marden Mill.

Before the suppression of Tynemouth Priory in 1539 by Henry VIII, the land on which Cullercoats stands appears to have been without any established settlement. Marden Mill was in the tenure of Robert and John Dove at a yearly rent of £9 0s 8d.

In 1600 a close containing two acres of pasture is mentioned in a survey and the area was called *Culvercoats*. The name continues to originate from the Anglo-Saxon name for dove cote that was built at Marden Close. This is the second time that the corruption of the current name of the village is mentioned although Ralph Delaval of Tynemouth had named the area *Culler Corners* in 1606 when he surrendered the land to his brother Peter Delaval. The place was known at this time as Arnolds Close alias Marden Close. The boundaries of this close were precisely defined as those of the present village of Cullercoats.

Cullercoats does not appear in Speede's map of Northumberland, which was published in 1610 though Whitley, Monkseaton, Earsdon, Hartley and other villages are clearly indicated.

By 1621 the area continued its long association with the Dove family when Thomas Dove of Whitley bought the land. Thomas Dove was one of the Tynemouth Four and Twenty in 1645, which was an early form of parish council and magisterial system, whose roots were in medieval times. Membership of such an elite group was highly prized, carried much status and was generally considered to be protestant in make-up. However, this was a time of religious questioning and the Dove family looked elsewhere for spiritual and religious enlightenment. They became nonconformists and started a Quaker movement. This angered the established church and John Dove and William Dove, sons of Thomas Dove, were imprisoned in Tynemouth Barracks for attending a Quaker meeting in 1661. However, their faith remained strong and by

1662 they had taken a piece of land at the north of John Street (formerly known as Back Lane) as a private burial ground, which remained there until 1818.

The first person to be buried there was a Joanna Linton but her resting place was soon disturbed. Her father died two years after her internment and the family objected to her being buried in non-consecrated ground. Guarded by soldiers the family removed her remains and reburied her in the graveyard at Tynemouth Church.

Not all the Doves were influenced by the teachings of George Fox. Robert Dove, brother of John and William Dove, remained a gentleman of the Four and Twenty.

Even as late as 1654 Cullercoats was of so little importance that it was omitted from Holler's map of the Tyne engraved for Ralph Gardner's *England's Grievance Discovered in relation to the Coal Trade*.

Nancy's Yard which was close to 'Sparrow Hall'.

In 1676 Thomas Dove, John Carr of Newcastle, John Rogers of Denton and Henry Hudson of Newbiggin became partners in Whitley Colliery. The following year a wooden pier was built at Cullercoats near to the present lifeboat station to export coal. This was a joint venture with the lease holders of Whitley Colliery and Lady Elizabeth Percy. Lady Percy was the only surviving child and sole heiress of Jocelyn, eleventh and last Earl of Northumberland. At this time, in a petition to the Lord Treasurer seeking permission for the export of coal from a pier at Cullercoats, Lady Percy referred to Cullercoats as *Caller Coates*. The petition was granted and the port was put under the charge of the Custom House Officer at Blyth. The wooden pier took five years to build at a cost of £3,013 13s 6d. In the same year the first two salt pans were started in Cullercoats Bay.

John Dove is credited with being concerned with building one of the earliest waggonways constructed in Northumberland. The waggonway, which was constructed of rails set on sleepers, was 15 yards in width and was built in 1677. In such waggonways lay the germ of the idea for the railway system. The construction of these waggonways was very primitive. The wheels and the rails on which they ran were made of wood and pulled by horses.

The waggonway ran from the Whitley and Monkseaton Collieries down by the south side of Marden Burn, past the north wall of the old burial ground along what became the main street of Cullercoats (Front Street) on the west side, past the Newcastle Arms until it reached the bank top where the Watch Tower stands today. Here the coals were shot over the bank to the vessels below.

The Dove family continued to dominate the affairs of Cullercoats and in 1682 they built a large Jacobean house that became colloquially known as 'Sparra (sparrow) Hall'. The locals christened the house thus as a result of misinterpreting the coats of arms, which was carved on a finial surmounting the east gable, which contained the initials of Thomas Dove and Elizabeth Dove together with a figure of a dove that the local population reinterpreted as a sparrow hawk. The hall when built stood in its own grounds, a little way back from the cliff and with an open view of the sea. It was exposed to the corroding forces of the Northerly gales and Easterly sea frets. Its latticed and mullioned windows needed to be made of stout materials to withstand such a hostile location. The house was described as an ordinary example of the Stuart period, three stories high with a centre gable projecting. Its charm lay its quaintness, its colouring and its pantile roof of varying shades of red. It certainly worked, as the house survived until 1979 when it was demolished as part of the development of Cullercoats.

Sometime between 1681 and 1688 Captain Granville Collins in the yacht *Merlin* made a survey of the coast of Great Britain, which was produced, in a large folio titled *Great Britain's Coasting Pilot*. Published in part in 1685 the chart of the Tyne and the surrounding area clearly identifies *Collar Coates* and *Whitley Pitts* as prominent landmarks. Cullercoats is described as:

Collar Coates

Is a Pier that lieth a mile or more from Tinmouth Castle to the Northward and is a Pier where vessels enter at high water and to load coals and lie dry at low water. The going in of this place is between several rocks. The way in is beacon'd.

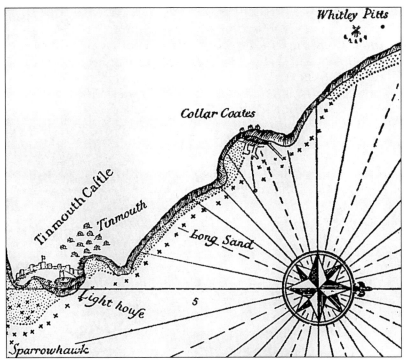

A copy of the maritime chart produced by Captain Granville Collins between 1681-84.

On 6th July 1690 Cullercoats was created a distinct township by an order made at the Quarter Sessions where: 'it is ordered that it (Cullercoats) be made a district constabulary in itself.' William Richardson was sworn in as the petty constable.

The coal and salt trade continued to flourish and by this time the original two salt pans erected in 1677 had increased by a further 17 – 7 north and 10 south of the bay in the Smugglers Cove area. Much of the coal mined at this time was of poor quality so rather than throw it away they sold it to the owners of the salt pans.

Salt was a valuable and precious commodity in the days when there was no freezing or canning. Salt was used to preserve fish, meat and vegetables for the winter. As well as being exported by sea, salt was transported away from the village by pack horse into the countryside along well recognised routes, which became known as Salter's Road and Salter's Bridge in Gosforth and Salter's Gate at Alnwick.

Salt is extracted from sea water by the age-old method of evaporation that leaves the residual salt crystals. Salt water was pumped to a huge cistern where the water was allowed to settle to clear it of mud and sand before it was allowed to run into the salt pans. Two tiers of shallow pans 15 feet long, 12 feet wide and 16 feet in depth, each containing 1,400 gallons of sea water were heated to boiling point by a coal furnace which used the cheap, locally available coal. The sea water was pumped into the upper pan, boiled and topped up three times until the brine was very strong. The liquid was then run off into the lower pans and allowed to cool. Whilst lukewarm the water was clarified using the white of eggs, sheep and black cattle blood. The pans were then filled up for a second, third and fourth time, the water clarified and boiled as before and as the water evaporated minute salt crystals or grains sank to the bottom. The salt crystals were then scraped from the pan, boxed on shelves for up to four days whilst they dried out and were then bagged for sale. The whole process from the first filling until the abstraction of the salt crystals took about twenty-four hours.

Salt making established Cullercoats, as a place of some importance in the North East but this is a little known fact. Ask anyone in the North East about Cullercoats and what it is known for and they will undoubtedly reply – fish.

In 1708 2,180 tons of salt was shipped from the small wooden pier, which yielded a profit of £538.

In 1710 the wooden pier was severely damaged in a storm and this disaster was the first of a series of reverses which the port was to experience. The disastrous Jacobean Uprising of 1715 unsettled the country and prejudiced all trades and industries. For some time after the suppression of the Uprising all Papists, Quakers and suspected persons were kept under strict surveillance and trade stifled.

Some idea of the trade that was done can be determined by examining the Custom Book at the Port of Blyth. Between 7th August 1723 and 6th August 1724 seventy-eight vessels cleared the harbour with coal bound for foreign parts. The first vessel that is mentioned as clearing coastwise was the *St Michael* of London with 100 tons of salt bound for the capital. In addition to the coal, in 1724 vessels carried 758 tons of salt and, in 1725, 668 tons of salt. The sailing colliers were of 230 tons each and two or three ships could be loaded during one high tide.

In the year 2002 it is difficult to believe that Cullercoats was once a thriving port, visited by foreign schooners of this type looking for cargoes of coal and salt.

Colliery 'Geordie' Brigs, similar to this vessel, the *Hilda*, were regular visitors to Cullercoats Bay.

Oats and wool were also exported and it is recorded that on one voyage 161 tons of wool was shipped in the *George and John*. The last clearance of a large sailing ship from Cullercoats was the *Fortune*, of Whitby, which cleared the harbour on the 18th July 1726 with a cargo of 21 tons of salt.

However, this commercial prosperity was short lived. By 1724 the Whitley and Cullercoats collieries were closed and salt exports ceased a year later in 1725 when the salt pans were moved to Blyth.

The first public house was built in Front Street in 1746 and named the Ship Inn.

Despite its small size as a harbour, Cullercoats also had its own registered sailing ships. On 16th August 1755 the *Newcastle Journal* reported the loss of the *Triton* of Cullercoats two weeks earlier whilst *en route* to Hamburg in ballast. The master of the vessel, George Heslop, was lost but fortunately the crew took to the long boat and were rescued after 16 hours at sea.

By the middle of the eighteenth century Cullercoats was a sleepy hamlet, whose residents eked out a precarious living from the sea. Most had turned to fishing but, given the dangers of the North Sea, many others had embraced smuggling as a way of making easy money.

In 1768 Captain Thomas Armstrong, a Customs Officer, built Cliff House. The history of the house is detailed in a separate section.

A large stone house was built next to the Newcastle Arms on Front Street in 1777. This was a grand house of classic character. In 1819 following the death of the owner, Mrs Coward, in her 85th year, it appeared for sale in the *Newcastle Courant*. The house was described as follows: 'An elegant stone faced house (pleasantly situated in Cullercoats containing eleven fire-rooms, three other rooms, a large garret, three stalled stable, a brew house, a gig house, and various other outbuildings, with a separate passage thereto, a garden and several courtyards.' Unfortunately the price of the house was not mentioned.

The Newcastle Arms, Front Street.

At the beginning of the nineteenth century coal mining at the redundant Whitley and Cullercoats workings started up again. However, by 1848 coal mining once again became unprofitable and the mines finally closed for good. This closure coincided with the period when the piers, which still stand today, were rebuilt.

Cullercoats was firmly established by the beginning of the nineteenth century and a journal of the important, tragic, trivial and sometimes amusing events now follows.

A JOURNAL OF EVENTS
IN CULLERCOATS, FROM
1800 UNTIL 1979

A 34-seat chain driven Fiat Charabanc, owned by the North Eastern Railway, ready for a day's outing in September 1908. PC Dixon is on the left and PC James Colpitts is on the right, both of whom resided in Hudleston Street.

This journal, which commences in 1800, does not seek to cover every eventuality and in some instances omits events to prevent any embarrassment to living relatives. However, there are some instances when the importance of the event is such that it is included, and where the account given is in the public domain. All of the events described have been reported in newspapers, magazines or in research documents.

An early engraving of Cullercoats, *circa* 1775.

In 1801 the population of Cullercoats was 452.

On 23rd December 1805 the residents of Cullercoats enjoyed an early Christmas present when a cask of gin was washed ashore. The *Newcastle Courant* describes the scene, 'Last week a cask of gin was driven on shore near Cullercoats (probably part of a smuggler's cargo). Those who found it knocked out one of the ends, made everyone welcome to drink what they pleased, and served it out plentifully to those who brought vessels to carry it away. Numbers were lying drunk and others rolling about the cask for the greater part of the day. One young man, who had been among the group, went into an adjoining field where he fell asleep and was found dead the next morning.' Some party.

Salt water Baths were considered to be beneficial to the health and in 1807 Richard Armstrong built 4 salt water bathrooms on the site now occupied by the Dove Marine Laboratory. Each bathroom had a separate dressing room. The bathhouse seemed to be in constant danger but unexpectedly not from the sea. Apparently the local inhabitants had no use for the baths, but the banks behind the baths held seams of coal, which the poorest dug into with little regard for the danger of the falls of earth on to the buildings below.

It is a matter of conjecture whether John Christie, also reportedly called Ramsay, saw the building of the new baths, as he died the same year aged 115 years. Christie was one of a number of people who lived into their hundreds at the first part of the nineteenth century. It is reported that he had all his faculties up until shortly before he died. He had served as a cabin boy aboard one of the ships under the command of Sir George Rooke when they took Gibraltar in 1704. An obituary notice placed in the *Newcastle Magazine* described Christie: 'an eccentric character, well known to the visitors of that place (Cullercoats).' It went on to describe Christie, as 'he is understood to have lost an eye and one arm in an engagement with the celebrated Paul Jones.' John Paul Jones was an American privateer who roamed the seas around England and Scotland during the American War of Independence attacking and looting English vessels. Christie was known as the 'laird.'

On the 30th May 1811 four Frenchmen, prisoners of war who had escaped from Edinburgh Castle nineteen days earlier, were caught trying to board an American ship at anchor off Cullercoats Bay. They were imprisoned at the House of Correction in Tynemouth.

In 1811 the population had risen by two over the previous ten years to 454. By 1821 the population had jumped to 536 where it remained constant over the next ten years.

The killing of whales has been a very emotive subject for the past three decades but it is a little known fact that between 1750 and 1850 the North East of England was one of the most important centres of the British whaling enterprise. From Berwick to Whitby, stoutly-built whaling ships, sailed annually to the Artic grounds in search of the Greenland Whale. These trips were long and dangerous with physical discomfort that we can hardly imagine. Their voyages sustained a shore-based processing and distribution industry of considerable value.

Hunting whales from open boats with a hand held harpoon in sub zero temperatures was not a venture for the faint hearted. It called for specialist skills of the men who hunted the whales, who were known as the 'Greenlanders', and the North East of England was renowned for them. These rough and ready men, who were revered for their nautical skills, acquired a folk hero status amongst their maritime communities.

Whale meat was rendered down by placing the blubber in large vats, which were heated so that the blubber turned to oil. The whale oil was used to make soap and to light the street lamps.

The *Camden* was a Whitby whaling ship, built in 1813, and was one of the largest whalers to sail from that port. Her master was John Armstrong, aged 43 years, an experienced whaleman from one of the oldest families in Cullercoats.

Camden's maiden whaling voyage in 1833 under his command was a great success, but subsequent voyages, with the exception of 1835, were poor. Despite the fact that the *Camden* had an experienced crew she returned empty to her homeport of Whitby in 1836 and 1837. Her owners, the Chapman family, withdrew her from service after only five voyages.

The history of this small village is nothing if not diversified. On 28th October 1826 an 'affair of honour' took place on Cullercoats Beach between Mr Keating, an officer of the 83rd Regiment, and Lieutenant Whateley RM. The cause of the quarrel is not known but it was reported in the *Newcastle Chronicle* as very trivial. Each antagonist fired two shots, which all missed their intended targets. It was then considered that honour was even on both sides and presumably both men returned to their army duties. It is hoped that the soldiers and sailors under their command were better marksmen.

Victoria Crescent was built in the year 1837 and replaced a number of small cottages known as Fisher Row. This picture is of Victoria Crescent at the turn of the twentieth century. The tram did not run along the sea front at this point and turned inland towards Whitley Bay.

The local newspapers tended to print any gossip or scandal and on 5th December 1840 the *Port of Tyne Pilot* reported the following story in the eloquent language so popular at the time.

'Peggy Robinson, known by the soubriquet (nickname) of the 'Queen of Cullercoats' charged three of the nymphs of that far famed marine village with assaulting her. She stated her case with great precision and with much force and underwent a cross examination by

Mr Joseph Laing who appeared fore the defendants that excited a great deal of mirth but she acquitted herself in a very masterly manner. Her husband too and an Irish boy also stood with much *éclat* against the cross examination of Mr Laing. We do not think it is worthwhile to occupy our columns by detailing the case. Two of the persons charged (named Lyal) were acquitted and the third, a married woman named Matthews was bound over to keep the peace as were the 'Queen' and the husband.'

Dove Cottage or Sparrow Hall stood alone for about a century but gradually a number of houses used as fishermen's cottages were built as Cullercoats thrived. Browns Buildings were built in 1838 on the west side of Front Street and epitomised a typical row of fishermen's cottages. Gathered about the entrance to the one-bedroomed cottages, the fisherfolk kept their lobster pots, creels, and wooden barrels with their layers of coarse salt rock for the once plentiful herring. Through the open doors quaint interiors were revealed, typically furnished with an old four-poster bed, chairs and table, the walls hung with cheap prints, the chimneypiece ornamented with brass candlesticks and china dogs.

Old Houses, Cullercoats.

The fishermen's cottages in Front Street numbered 27-33, which are frequently misnamed, Browns Buildings. The large three-storey building at the end of the cottages is No 26, which during its life was a bakery and a drapers for a period of time.

Browns Buildings were the nine cottages at the rear of the fishermen's cottages situated at 27-33 Front Street. It is believed that they took their name from the local baker called Brown who had premises on Front Street.

In 1842 the population suddenly jumped to 738.

In 1848 the piers at Cullercoats, as you see them today, were built by way of public subscription with substantial donations being made by the Duke of Northumberland and the Corporation of Newcastle.

By 1850 a school had been built in Back Lane (now called John Street) at a cost of £400 raised by public subscription. The Duke of Northumberland donated the land. This cannot have been the first school as £100 was raised on 21st July 1821 through a bazaar at the Star and Garter public house, Tynemouth.

It is surprising that despite the size of the population and the growth of Cullercoats that no running water or sewage system was in existence in 1851. A report in 1851, which concentrated mainly on North Shields, and which was published by the General Board of Health, makes for grim reading. Whilst Cullercoats residents were enjoying a reasonably healthy, if hard life, the rate of mortality in North Shields was high with cholera endemic in certain areas. In North Shields the instances of cholera were four times higher than in Tynemouth and none are recorded for Cullercoats.

In the first fifty years of the nineteenth century six people lived beyond the age of 100 years but this longevity of life was not replicated in North Shields. At this time North Shields had a population of 21,710 persons or 5,590 families living in 74 streets. For the use of these families there was on average one privy (toilet) for every five families and the Low Town was extremely unhealthy with open sewers, dung heaps, offal and effluent thrown out on to the streets.

Crime was also extremely high in North Shields and in comparative terms was extremely low and minor in Cullercoats. Most of the transgressions were when alcohol clouded the vision or were minor squabbles between neighbours.

A tranquil Cullercoats Bay, *circa* 1890.

Compare this with a report submitted by Police Superintendent Robert Mitchell on the condition of the Lodging Houses in North Shields dated 25th January 1850.

'In consequence of the numerous complaints which were daily made to me respecting the great number of vagrants who were carrying on an extensive system of begging and petty theft in the town, I was induced to make an inspection of the lodging houses frequented by persons of this character and the results of my inquiries convinced me that so long as these receptacles of thieves, vagabonds and prostitutes are allowed to exist there cannot be any effectual stop put to thieving and begging in the town. I find that there are 23 houses, which none but these characters frequent. I likewise ascertained that the beggars go out in the morning and do not return until a late hour at night; and when they do return they are loaded with the day's collection of begging and pilfering. I also ascertained that any piece of stolen property that they may bring with them is immediately despatched to a marine store shop and there converted to money. I have ascertained that these shops afford every disposal of stolen property. I am convinced that parties selling articles at such places receive but a small portion of the value of what they sell. I have also ascertained that persons disposing of goods in this way may redeem them at the expiration of one week by paying 40 or 50 per cent on the amount advanced on them. Generally speaking beggars realize a larger income weekly and live upon a better fare than does the honest labouring man. In one house, the notorious 'Sally Joyce's' on the Steam Mill Bank, I found one night eleven persons who had been living for a considerable period of time on no other visible means other that of pilfering. The most of them had been convicted thieves and were associates of thieves. They were regaling themselves with a piece of beef, eggs, tea and some hot whisky toddy. The apartments of the house were in the filthiest condition that could be imagined, it beggars description. In one of the cupboards, having occasion to search for some stolen property, there was a deposit of human filth. There were four beds in the room, three persons to a bed, and behind the beds was a hen roast with a deposit of filth. The effluvium from the room was most overpowering. Connecting the apartment with the room above was a trap door by which a person could escape from one apartment to another when pursued by the police. The description for the house, its occupants and its filthy condition would nearly answer for the other three and twenty. The people frequenting such places are generally strong, able-bodied subjects, who will not work and so long as they are permitted to stop in town and these dens of iniquity are permitted to be kept open for them; we cannot expect much diminution of crime for our population. It were unnecessary to describe the conditions of the lanes and courts in which these houses are situate but it will suffice to say that in the absence of any sanitary regulations they are generally kept in the most filthy and foul conditions, every description of filth is thrown into them, and as the water is allow to stagnate in the gutters it is clear that a most pestiferous influence must pervade the neighbourhood, engendered both in the houses and in the streets affecting the respectable inhabitants within the immediate proximity of these places and proving most injurious to the health of the town generally. I observed no personal cleanliness, no pumps, few pants or any means of plentiful water.'

This depressing picture did not apply to Cullercoats but the report did document that Cullercoats had no running water and was serviced by three wells in the Marden Burn area. There was no sewage system and most residents washed in the sea.

Census returns commenced in 1841 and take place every 10 years. In 1861 the returns showed 156 fishermen, 16 fisherwomen, 2 baitresses aged 14 years, 6 pilots four of whom were also fishermen, 18 mariners and a pilot's widow living in Cullercoats. The total population now stood at 660 and was served by four public houses – two Ship Inns, the Queens Head and the Newcastle Arms (formerly the Hope and Anchor.) Twenty-one households had servants and a solicitor and a barrister lived in the larger houses.

One of the most tragic shipwrecks, which is immortalised on canvas by the painter John Charlton (The Women, 1904), concerned the wreck of the colliery brig the *Lovely Nelly* on New Year's morning 1861. The *Lovely Nelly* was by now an aged vessel and must have been approaching the end of her life. In 1861 she was in her 57th year.

The *Lovely Nelly* regularly plied her trade between Seaham and London carrying coal and on this fateful day she had originally been bound for London when she sprang a serious leak. The ship made to return to Seaham but was driven north by gale force winds. Unable to enter the Tyne the ship was observed at Tynemouth flying a signal of distress struggling northward but with difficulty and driving towards the shore. A severe tempest with rain and snow was blowing and the Seaham vessel was heavily laden. The coastguard men, who followed her along the shore, observed her plight. The local population turned out to join them so that a large number of onlookers manned each headland.

The *Lovely Nelly* struggled northward past Cullercoats but became more and more unmanageable as some of her sails were blown away and the heavy seas broke around and over her. The master of the vessel then determined that his best chance of survival was to drive the vessel ashore on Whitley Sands and altered course. She struck the rocks and became wrecked three quarters of a mile offshore. The vessel was out of range of any rocket apparatus and Cullercoats lifeboat was summoned.

Cullercoats Bay at the time of the tragedy of the *Lovely Nelly*. The picture can be dated as pre-1879 as there is no Watch Tower.

The Cullercoats lifeboat *Percy* was physically manhandled out of the station and six sturdy horses attached to the carriage. The horses and the men and women of Cullercoats strained with all their might to get the lifeboat onto Whitley Sands where the crew attempted a dangerous rescue. The lifeboat men rowed out to the *Lovely Nelly*, which was now lying broadside to the incoming waves. The decks were awash and the crew had taken to the rigging. Such was the ferocity of the sea; waves were breaking over her masts. The lifeboat managed to get alongside the ship and some of the crew scrambled aboard the lifeboat. Three men fell into the sea but two of them were immediately rescued. A third man fell into the sea to what seemed certain death but a strong arm of a lifeboat man managed to drag him aboard by his hair before he drowned.

One person remained on board, little Tommy Thompson, the cabin boy who was high in the rigging and would not let go. Time and again the lifeboat tried to rescue little Tommy but was driven back by the huge seas. His plaintiff cries of despair urged the lifeboat men onwards but as the vessel started to break up they were forced to abandon their efforts and pull away. Little Tommy was seen to fall into the sea and the lifeboat rushed to his aid. Twice he surfaced with hands clasped as if in prayer and then he disappeared into the foam and was swept away to his death.

Fifteen lifeboat men manning ten oars did everything that was humanely possible to save little Tommy Thompson in weather conditions that few of us can imagine. Their frustration and anguish at being so close but so helpless to save his life we can only imagine.

The body of little Tommy Thompson was recovered the next day. He was buried in St John's Church, Seaham.

There are times in bad weather, when the sea is raging and the wind howling, that you can imagine his plaintive cries for help. Spare a thought for little Tommy Thompson, his short life and his awful fate.

In 1864 the railway arrived in Cullercoats when the Blyth and Tyne Railway opened Cullercoats Station on Mast Lane. The line was moved nearer to the coast in 1882 and the present railway station opened in Station Road.

A reef that has claimed many a vessel surrounds the headland which protects Cullercoats haven from the north, Browns Point. It was here that the barque *Warrior* came ashore on 29th October 1864, the steamer *Warkworth Castle* on 15th November 1876 which went to pieces on New Year's Day 1877 and the brig *Astley* on 26th October 1887.

The *Warrior* was caught in a gale from the North East when all along the coast the seas were running very high. All vessels made for ports of refuge in which to shelter out the storm. At 9 pm *Warrior*, which was in ballast from Hamburg to the Tyne, tried to make for the Tyne entrance but was driven ashore. She fired her signals of distress but was lying in such a position on the reef that the lifeboat could not reach her. The rocket apparatus was used to rescue the crew and all crewmembers were saved. As the last man was being landed with the sling life buoy the vessel started to break up and became a total wreck.

The *Warkworth Castle* was a North Shields registered ship of 746 gross tonnage. Near to midnight on 15th November 1876, whilst *en route* from London to Newcastle where she was to pick up a cargo bound for Constantinople, she came ashore in dense fog. The coastguard had not seen her progress and the first indications that she had come ashore was when the fishermen of Cullercoats heard the cries for help from the boat. The Cullercoats Life Brigade rescued all twenty-two crew together with the captain's wife and four children.

The *Astley* had been in ballast from Gluckstadt to her homeport of Hartlepool when she was seen close to shore in the breakers off Tynemouth. The *Astley* drove high up on to the rocks and the Cullercoats Life Brigade, who had been following the progress of the ship with some concern since she had been sighted off the mouth of the Tyne, fired two rockets over her. The crew consisting of five men and a boy were then hauled ashore by means of the running gear (breeches buoy). One of the crewmembers refused to leave the stricken vessel without his pet dog and cat and he was seen running around the decks gathering up his pets. He succeeded in getting both and was safely rescued with the cat in one arm and the dog in the other.

Cullercoats Volunteer Life Brigade had been formed in the early part of 1865 and was the second Brigade enrolled in the United Kingdom, the first being its close cousin the Tynemouth Volunteer Life Brigade. At the time it was formed it had between 60 and 70 volunteers, the vast majority of them were local fishermen. The duty of the Life Brigade was to assist the Coastguard in their rescue endeavours to save lives due to shipwreck by means of rocket apparatus.

Cullercoats Volunteer Life Brigade House, which became the Rocket Garage, *circa* 1955.

In order to effectively discharge their duties it was necessary to provide an efficient watch, in times of bad weather, both night and day. This they initially did in the open, whilst exposed to the full fury of bad weather, with little more than a stone wall for shelter.

The Watch Tower was eventually built in 1879 at the spot where Cullercoats fisherfolk had always assembled to watch the fishing boats go out and come back into the bay, and in bad weather where many stood weary and anxious awaiting the return of their fathers, sons, husbands and brothers. The Watch Tower is one of the best-known landmarks in the area, standing as it does, keeping its vigil from the headland.

The Watch Tower was financed through the Board of Trade and by local charity. However, the clock was donated by a philanthropic individual and had originally resided in a house just north of the Watch Tower. For many years the house stood with a gaping hole where the clock had once resided.

Clock House, like a sightless Cyclops, being battered by the waves after giving up its clock to the Watch House.

The Corporation of Tynemouth undertook to put the works in order, fit a new dial, new striking works and put a light into the belfry where it is housed. The tower originally had a working bell that was used in foggy weather but the bell no longer sounds today

The Bay Hotel holds a commanding position on the sea front at Cullercoats with its splendid views over the bay. Built in April 1870 the hotel was originally called the Hudleston Arms and at that time stood on the corner of the busiest street in Cullercoats – Hudleston Street. The establishment was described as being most comfortably furnished with good stabling and a coach house attached to the hotel. At the time of the opening it was being contemplated as to whether to run an omnibus between the hotel and Tynemouth during the summer months.

Cullercoats Volunteer Life Brigade Look-out House built in 1879.

Opposite St George's Church is a small promontory that was known even before the building of the church as George's Point although the 1865 Ordinance Survey map details it as Tynemouth North Point. Close to this point is the Ninety Fathom Dyke, which is a geological fault and stretching out from this point are the reef of rocks known as the Saddle Rocks, Crab Hill and Bear's Back.

On 8th December 1870 a large barque called the *City of Bristol* met her doom on the Bear's Back. The 539-ton ship belonging to South Shields was on passage with chalk ballast from London to Shields. The *Amalie* of Stavanger, whose crew were fortunately rescued by the Tynemouth lifeboat, followed her a few hours later. A few years later these wrecks were joined by another.

These were not the only vessels to succumb to the bad weather at this time. The *Mary Fenwick* of South Shields was wrecked at Amble. The steamship *Eagle* was driven ashore at the Herd Sands, South Shields. However, the most tragic wreck claimed the lives of seven of the same family. The 85-ton Boston schooner *Samuel Bernard* was seen running for the Tyne in heavy seas. She had almost made it into the refuge of the river when she was hit amidships by a huge wave, which rolled her over. She disappeared from view, never to reappear. The crewmembers, who were the master of the vessel, his wife and five children, all perished.

Cullercoats Bay before the Watch Tower was built. At this time the cobles used to be kept on the large field opposite Beverley Terrace.

In 1872 the Corporation of Tynemouth decided to extend John Street to the Marden Burn in order to join it to Whitley Lane (now Road). The Quaker burial ground, which Thomas Dove had opened, lay in its path in a much-neglected state. The sanction of the Society of Friends was obtained and the bones and tombstones were moved to Preston Cemetery where they rest in peace today. The names and the dates of their deaths were recorded from their tombstones, many of which had been severely eroded:

Thomas Airey	27th October 1675
Son of Henry Airey	4th November 167?
Robert Curry	20th September 1680
Daughter of Robert Curry	19th August 1680
Hannah Dove, wife of John Dove	1684
Francis, daughter of Thomas Dove	July 1683 or 1688
John Willoby	1689
Ellenor Dove, wife of Thomas Dove	2nd March 16??
Eliner Dove, wife of William Dove	(unreadable)
Elizabeth, daughter of John Buston	1695
Doratha Frost, wife of John Frost	26th February 1697
Margaret Haddock, wife of Zephaniah Haddock	5th April 1699
Martha Haslem, wife of Lawrence Haslem	13th December 1703
John Buston	30th November 1710

In 1880 Cullercoats had some 80 cobles in the harbour and the population now neared 2,000 including visitors.

One of the most prominent landmarks in Cullercoats, which continues to dominate the skyline, is St George's Church with its 180 foot spire situated on the south boundary of the village. The church was built between 1882 and 1884 at a cost of around £30,000 by the Duke of Northumberland as a memorial to his father George Percy, the fifth Duke of Northumberland. The church was designed in the style of the thirteenth century.

St George's Church, built 1882-84.

In the same year that the building of St George's commenced the North Eastern Railway Company opened its new coastline route and the old Whitley waggonway route was abandoned save for the transport of coal.

The Bear's Back claimed another wreck on 12th January 1883 when a large steam ship drove ashore. At just past midnight Police Sergeant Scott, on night duty at Tynemouth, was walking along the sea front to meet a constable in Cullercoats when he observed a blue light being waved from a vessel close to shore. The night was dark but the heavy seas of the previous two days had now lessened. The officer saw the vessel had run aground immediately in front of St George's Church, which was under construction. The vessel was so close to the shore that he could hear people shouting on board and then shortly after that signals of distress were fired.

The alarm was quickly raised and spread from house to house until the whole of the village was made aware of the wreck. The vessel was found to be the *Libelle*, *en route* from Bergen to Hamburg in ballast, carrying a crew of twenty-one people and eight passengers. The Cullercoats lifeboat rescued everyone from the boat despite the fact that the *Libelle* was lying broadside on to the sea and the waves were breaking over her decks.

Anyone with a basic knowledge of geography knows that the Tyne is not on the route from Bergen to Hamburg, although one account does suggest that she was bound for the Tyne. It would appear that after leaving Bergen in a storm the steering gear of the *Libelle* failed and she was blown across the North Sea before coming to rest at Cullercoats. The *Libelle* was a total loss and was eventually refloated, towed into the Tyne and scrapped.

Just after 4 am on 25th October 1885 an exceptionally high tide helped by strong winds breached the breakwater on the north side of Cullercoats Bay. One hundred tons of stone were hurled 10 to 15 feet by the force of the water. The tide and the height of the sea can be judged by the fact that an old wreck, which formerly lay near St Mary's Island, was carried half a mile down the coast line and dumped, keel upwards at the Brier Dene Burn, Whitley Bay.

In 1890 a charismatic and successful entrepreneur patronised the village through the acquisition of Monks Haven. Sir James Knott was born in January 1855 the son of a Customs Officer.

In 1864 after some eight years in the Customs service his father became an innkeeper taking the Old Inn in Nile Street, North Shields. Within a few years he changed the business from an inn into a wine and spirit merchants.

James attended school in Howard Street, North Shields, and when he left he went to work on Newcastle Quayside in the offices of Borries,

Sir James Knott.

Craig and Company, who were merchants and shipbrokers. Twelve to eighteen months before he got married he went into partnership with a Newcastle shipbroker, James Thompson & Co, whose office was in Burn Bank. This was one of the chares leading back from the river where the new Newcastle Crown Courts now stand.

The brig *Pearl* was the first ship that James Knott had a financial interest in. Not a lot is known about the *Pearl* other than she was a typical sailing collier brig and at 45 years old, somewhat near the end of her working life when she came under his control. His early ventures into shipowning were not without its drawbacks. His next acquisition, the 32-year-old brig *Rival*, acquired on 29th November

1879, was wrecked a month later on 28th December 1879. The next ship lasted about six months and was 35 years old.

However, he steadily made progress and on 3rd March 1881 he launched a new steamship named *Saxon Prince*. This was the start of the very successful Prince Line. In 1916 the business was sold as a going concern for £3,000,000, comprising a fleet of 37 modern steamships.

In 1890 a potted biography of James Knott describes him as a man of energy, ability and sound business habits and part of the secret of his success was his careful choice of officers and the strict discipline, which prevailed at head office. All his ship masters sailed with the grim warning in front of them: 'All accidents are the result of carelessness.' Whether this legend was a fixture in the wheel house or a verbal instruction is not known. A bonus was given to masters who ran their vessels successfully for twelve months, but on the other hand, in case of collision or stranding, an officer was compelled to resign. The crewmembers of his ships with long service received a bonus payment of five shillings per month, for this payment they had to wear the company's cap with the ship's name on a ribbon and a jersey with Prince Line in white letters on the chest.

James married Margaret Annie Garbutt in 1878, the daughter of the late Thomas Garbutt, a Wesleyan minister, and it was suggested that James become involved with the Wesleyan church as a sort of reaction to his father's business 'the demon drink'.

About 1890 the family moved from the house in Alma Place in North Shields to The Manor House in Jesmond, where they had nine servants.

Another house they acquired about this time was an attractive terraced house in Cullercoats called the 'Monks Haven'. The Knotts were now in the two-home league and this was probably more of a weekend 'cottage'. It is now a Methodist retirement home. A fine

The weekend residence of Sir James Knott, now a retirement home for the elderly.

copper relief still stands in the entrance hall of a Cullercoats fishwife with her creel on her back and is a reminder that James and his wife had a soft spot for Cullercoats fisherfolk. The copper relief is supposed to depict Polly Donkin. The family were very fond of Cullercoats and supportive of the locals, their traditions and heritage.

In the days when most people ate a proper lunch, the Cullercoats fishwives used the train to get to Newcastle before lunch to sell their fish. When the new electric train service between the coast and Newcastle started around 1903, the fishwives were compelled to use a special train. They then had a problem if their husband's boat was late in due to the weather as they missed their special train and the chance of selling their fish in Newcastle. James Knott made successful representation to the North Eastern Railway Company, which allowed them to travel in the guards van of the electric train with their fresh fish.

James Knott was obviously a man who liked to get his own way and did not like to lose. A number of anecdotal stories are common knowledge and are believed to be true. One of them is pertinent to Cullercoats relating to Monks Haven.

The local Borough Surveyor was asked to call at the Prince Line offices in Newcastle to discuss a proposal that James Knott had for a road improvement, which would have made it possible for Monks Haven to have a bigger front garden. The Borough Surveyor said that he could not agree to this plan at all, and so the meeting was terminated. As he was leaving the office he paused to look at a chart upon which the whereabouts of each Prince Line ship was indicated. James Knott asked him what he was looking for; he replied that he was interested in a particular ship on which his brother-in-law was chief engineer. 'You mean he was,' said James and promptly arranged for his chief engineer to be paid off abroad somewhere.

In the birthday honours of 1917 James Knott was created a baronet He died seventeen years later but his name lives on in the form of a number of charitable trusts.

Whilst it was always considered that fishing, as an occupation was dangerous, it would appear from a number of press reports that the North Eastern Railway line had its fair share of fatalities. In the early hours of Monday 17th March 1890 John Lisle, 63 years, a fisherman of back Simpson Street, was found dead on the lines four hundred yards south of Cullercoats Station. Both feet had been amputated and it was supposed that Lisle, who had been drinking in Tynemouth with some friends the evening before, had returned home by trespassing on the railway line when he had been run over by a train.

In 1899 the August Bank Holiday came late. By now Cullercoats was a popular holiday destination and had the day-trippers and weekenders stayed late they would have witnessed a spectacular sight. The *Fairy Maid* an 80 ton two-masted sailing ship belonging to Somerset, was bound for the Tyne in ballast from Amsterdam. Weather conditions were good but for some unknown reason shortly after 9 pm the *Fairy*

Maid steered an erratic course and missed the entrance to the Tyne. She drove up on Cullercoats Bay just beneath Cliff House were she remained stranded for some considerable time. Her crew of four were able to walk ashore.

The stranding of the *Fairy Maid* on Bank Holiday Monday, 1899. After some weeks she was eventually refloated and saved.

On Sunday 30th July 1900 George Alexander Wood, a hairdresser residing in Byker, Newcastle, was seeing a friend away from Cullercoats Railway Station when he fell between the platform and the moving carriage. He was cut in two.

In the same month of the above tragedy the *Shields Daily News* ran an advertisement for Gregg's new café in Saville Street, North Shields. Whilst the menu could not be described at extensive or 'haute cuisine' the restaurant offered the following wholesome fare which I have converted into present day money in brackets.

Ox Tail and Kidney Soup; Scotch Broth	3d	(1.5p)
Salmon and Green Peas	1s	(5p)
Roast Lamb	1s	(5p)
Roast Chicken	1s	(5p)
Roast Beef and Yorkshire Pudding	1s	(5p)
Milk, Sweet, Pastry, Stewed Fruit Puddings	3d	(1.5p)
Ices, Mineral waters etc	2d	(1p)

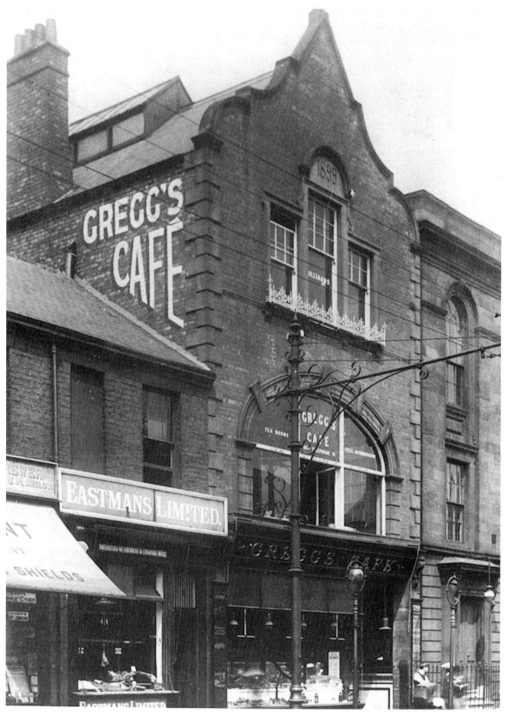

Gregg's Café, Saville Street, North Shields.

On 29th October 1900 a severe rainstorm hit the area and Cullercoats Railway Station was completely flooded, with the water reaching the level of the platforms. A train, which attempted to pass through the station, was brought to a sudden stop when the water extinguished the train's boiler fire. A number of carriages were derailed as they floated in the water.

A flooded Cullercoats Railway station, 1900.

Hudleston Street was one of the busiest streets in Cullercoats, full of shops and friendly folk who liked to be out and about exchanging news and views about their neighbours. This was fortunate for a police investigation into the most serious of all crimes – murder.

Joseph Ferguson resided at 53 Hudleston Street, Cullercoats, in September 1901 with his wife Mary. He had originally lodged at this address when his wife was married to John Miller, who had died leaving his wife financially secure. After a decent period of mourning he had married her some four and half years before his murder. Following this marriage, his wife Mary had changed her will and left her property and belongings to her new husband who was younger than her. Whether this was the cause of family discord is a matter of conjecture. The Miller family did not really fit into the make-up of the Cullercoats residents having been hawkers before settling in the village.

John Miller, 67 years, a showman with roundabouts on Tynemouth Sands was by marriage the stepson of Joseph Ferguson despite being older than his stepfather. John Robert Miller, 30 years, a musician of no fixed abode, was a nephew of John Miller.

Images of Hudleston Street

Hudleston Street at the time of the murder of Joseph Ferguson, *circa* 1905.

Miss Callus's shop in Hudleston Street, *circa* 1956. This shop sold everything and was stacked from floor to ceiling. Whenever a customer entered the shop Miss Callum would pop up like a genie out of a bottle from behind the counter.

An hour before the murder of Joseph Ferguson, John Miller and his nephew entered a shop in North Shields and bought a knife stating, that the nephew was a cook who went to sea. The knife was bought for 11 pence by the nephew and he was seen to put it in his overcoat pocket and hand some change to his uncle, John Robert Miller.

They must have made their way immediately to Cullercoats where both men were seen banging on the door of 55 Hudleston Street. John Robert Miller was standing to one side where the person opening the door could not see him. Once Joseph Ferguson opened the door, both men were seen to rush inside pushing Ferguson ahead of them.

Their behaviour had aroused local suspicion and shortly afterwards the younger Miller was heard to say as he left the house, 'You have worked me up to this pitch. You gave me the drink and you gave me the knife.' He was covered in blood. Shortly after this Joseph Ferguson was found dead in his house of stab wounds.

Members of the public held both Millers until the police arrived and the men were taken to North Shields Police Station. The younger Miller was by this time full of remorse and openly stated 'I done it. I done it. Take and hang me. I have murdered my uncle.' He was cautioned and continued to make his admissions. 'It is all right, I am going to die. I've done something to make me die. It's true I have committed murder. I will die a coward. Never before God had I any intention of doing it.'

The older Miller was obviously wilier as the admissions of guilt were being made in his presence. He told the police, 'I have nothing to do with the affair. I tried to prevent the affair but could not. I have as little to do with this as you have.'

Both men were charged with murder and the wheels of justice were better oiled in 1901 as both men appeared before the Newcastle Assize Court in November 1901. Both men pleaded Not Guilty in accordance with the law of the day, although, John Robert Miller qualified his plea by saying, 'I can't say that I am guilty.' During the time that capital punishment was in being an accused person was not allowed to plead Guilty to a capital offence. Both men were convicted and went to the gallows on Saturday 7th December 1901. John Miller was executed first, death being instantaneous. Just prior to his execution he stated 'Gentlemen I die an innocent man.' John Robert Miller was hung one and half hours later.

Another fatal accident occurred at Cullercoats Railway Station at 10 pm on Saturday 19th October 1901 when Samuel Smith of Philip Street, Newcastle, was found dead on the railway lines just after a train had departed. Both legs had been amputated and he died from his injuries. Smith had apparently tried to board the train as it was departing and was dragged on to the lines after he lost his footing.

Henry Foster, a bookmaker, of Percy Avenue, Cullercoats, fell foul of the law in the form of PC Darling, the local policeman, in June 1902. Foster was seen in Victoria Crescent, Cullercoats, at 4.30 in the afternoon using 'disgusting language'. He was advised to go home but became belligerent and advised the constable that he would do as he pleased. Foster was arrested for being drunk and disorderly and walked to Tynemouth Police Station where he offered to fight PC Darling. Foster appeared at North Shields Magistrates Court where he pleaded Not Guilty despite admitting that he had consumed between 8 and 10 glasses of sherry. Foster was found guilty and fined £1 with costs after it was revealed that this was his third conviction.

A tramcar in Mona Terrace outside of the first Life Brigade House.

A tramcar in John Street coming from Whitley Bay.

By 1904 two tramway companies were fully servicing a 12 mile route between Newcastle's Central Station and North Shields and on through Tynemouth, Cullercoats and Whitley Bay.

The process of the law enforcement in the courts is always worthy of examination. At North Shields Police Court on 7th January 1905 Robert Robson, 50 years of Station Road, Cullercoats, appeared before the bench for failing to pay maintenance to his wife. The following conversation was reported in the *Shields Daily News*:

Mr R.F. Kidd, Magistrates Clerk: 'Do you owe £20 under this order?

Defendant Robson: 'It is owing but I don't consider it owing now. I find this woman is not my wife.'

Mr Kidd: 'The order is in force. There is a proper way of getting it set aside. Have you any goods, which can be taken into distress?

Defendant: 'I can pay the amount due under protest. But she is not my wife, and I defy her to prove it.'

Mr Kidd: 'We have nothing to do with that this morning.'

Chairman of the Bench: 'You will be committed for two months. The committal will be suspended to see if you pay the money. If you don't you will go to prison and you can settle whether she is your wife or not after you come out.'

Obviously the rules of the court were more important and the order was to be obeyed. Whether Robson paid up or not or what his basis was for stating that his wife was not his wife is not known.

The Fishermen's Choir, *circa* 1886, outside of the Watch House with John Lisle on the far left in the back row.

The way of life in Cullercoats at the start of the twentieth century was something of a paradox. Crime was not of the endemic proportions of today but minor assaults, family squabbling and a degree of drunkenness was the order of the day. However, within the community there were many devout people.

John Lisle was a man described of 'great Christian character' who seeing the sin within the village and the need of the people took it upon himself to start a Fisherman's Mission. A building in Front Street was obtained with a meeting hall upstairs and Sundays saw the place packed to the doors. Following his death in 1912 his son, Albert Lisle, continued his father's work and a new Fisherman's Mission was built in Eskdale Terrace and opened in 1931. The Mission still continues today and carries out its evangelistic service that the founders started.

In April 1906 it was announced that a Marconi Radio Station was to be built upon Promontary Point. Masts of over 200 feet in height were to be erected and a wooden building, which would house the radio receiver, stood at the foot of the masts.

An aerial view of the Marconi Point radio station and aerials, which could be seen from miles away.

The railways continued to claim lives when another body was discovered on the lines between Cullercoats and Whitley Bay at 7.15 am on Thursday 4th October 1906. The body was identified as Mr James Newham, a sail maker of 144 Linskill Street, North Shields, and it was apparent that he had been run over by a train. An inquest concluded that Newham, a man in his seventies who was losing his mental faculties, had been run down by a train whilst trespassing on the line.

It would seem that bookmakers had a propensity to over indulge in the consumption of alcohol when Arthur Dickinson, 32 years of 74 Hudleston Street, Cullercoats, appeared before Tynemouth Borough Magistrates Court on Monday 14th March 1910 charged with being drunk and disorderly. PC Darling stated that Dickinson was found acting disorderly outside his father-in-law's house and was drunk. Upon arrest he became very violent and was put to the ground and restrained until another constable arrived to assist. A counter allegation was made by the defendant's wife that she had seen PC Darling kick at her husband whilst he was on the ground, but this was denied. Dickinson was found guilty and fined £1, this being his 21st appearance for drunkenness.

On 15th January 1913 the iron-built four-masted barque *California*, of 2,518 gross tons came ashore at St Mary's Island, Whitley Bay. The vessel had been laid up in the Tyne for a long time before a shipowner from Finland purchased it. The vessel had a crew of 27 men on board and with a part cargo of 800 tons of coal and 50 tons of pig iron was bound for Rotterdam where she was to pick up a further eleven crew members and sail for Calloa in South America.

The voyage stated off badly. An Easterly storm was raging with heavy snow and the master of the barque enlisted the help of the steam tug *Plover*. Even before she left the Tyne she collided with the quayside at Tyne Dock causing major damage to the dock but none to the ship. The *Plover* towed the ship northwards in bad conditions and for some reason the master of the tug determined that the master of the *California* wanted to return to the Tyne. This was not correct but as the tug attempted to return to the Tyne the towline parted and the barque drifted away. The *Plover* apparently searched for a few hours for the lost barque but could not find it in the snowstorms. They did see a wreck on St Mary's Island but did not think it was their charge.

Meanwhile the *California* had run ashore a quarter of a mile south of St Mary's Island at 1 am. As soon as she hit the rocks she heeled around and started to break up. Within five minutes all her lifeboats and deckhouses were washed away and the masts and rigging came down shortly afterwards. The seas were breaking over the vessel and three crewmembers were washed overboard to their deaths. The stricken vessel was not seen for 14 hours.

The Seaton Sluice Life Brigade affected rescue but the Cullercoats lifeboat, which had set off in atrocious conditions, was beaten back as she broke all but four of their oars. George Lisle, son of the coxswain of the lifeboat, was washed overboard but was fortunately hauled aboard again when the next wave carried him within arm's length of the lifeboat.

The bodies of the three seamen who were drowned were later recovered and lie buried in St Paul's Church, Whitley Bay.

The steamship *Rhodesian* of London went ashore during foggy weather at 3 am 20th March 1916 on the Bear's Back opposite St George's Church. In response to distress rockets and signals the Cullercoats lifeboat was launched and the crew safely taken off the vessel. The *Rhodesian* was firmly grounded and lay broadside to the sea. The vessel was scrapped where she came to rest.

It was almost at this same spot that the Norwegian barque *Inga* had went ashore during a November gale 15 years earlier. The *Inga* from Christiansand missed the Tyne lights in appalling weather and hit the rocks. Fifteen crewmembers perished but one 28-year-old man was fortunate to be washed ashore. The gales that assailed the coast over this three-day period between 12th and 14th November 1901 sank 27 ships and claimed over 100 lives.

Like everywhere in the land Cullercoats shared in the losses of young men during the First World War, 35 Cullercoats men were killed in action.

On 17th May 1923 a coble in the charge of Jack Armstrong of Cullercoats caught a 48 lb salmon, which was the largest salmon landed at North Shields Fish Quay for many years. The salmon measured 4 feet 3 inches and bidding started at 1s 3d (7p) per pound. The fish was eventually bought by a fishmonger from Jesmond for £3 18s 0d (£3.90p). The weight of the fish caused quite a stir, although it was attested in the local newspaper that within living memory two other salmon weighing 52 lbs had been caught within the preceding forty-five years.

The crime rate at Cullercoats continued to spiral and on 28th May 1925 May Turtle of 30 Simpson Street, Cullercoats, appeared before North Shields Magistrates Court charged with shaking a mat at 3.15 pm on 15th May to the annoyance of pedestrians. The police evidence showed that the defendant was told that mats should be shaken before 8 am to which she replied, 'That doesn't worry me,' and proceeded to brush and shake another mat covering the police constable in dust. Turtle pleaded guilty through ignorance of the law and was fined 4 shillings (20p).

One of the worst disasters to hit Cullercoats occurred just after 2 pm on 22nd April 1939 and was witnessed by thousands of people. The new Cullercoats motor lifeboat *Richard Silver Oliver*, the first of its kind at Cullercoats, was launched on exercise. The following crew and dignitaries were on board

Lionel Edward Robin Blakeney-Booth, honorary secretary of the station
Kenneth Leslie Biggar, 16 years, stepson of the above
Coxswain George Brunton
Second Coxswain John Redford Armstrong
Mechanic John Leonard Abel
Assistant Mechanic John Heddon Scott
Bowman Jacob Chisholm Brunton
RNLI District engineer John William Smith
Lifeboat man Andrew Oliver Tweedy
Lifeboat man James Gilbert Carmichael

The sea was rough with a spring tide running and there was a North Easterly gale. The *Richard Silver Oliver* went towards St Mary's Island where she turned and returned towards Cullercoats making for Tynemouth Piers where there was a nasty sea aggravated by the backwash from the Piers. The lifeboat successfully turned back for Cullercoats but ran close to the shore through the heavy breaking water. As she approached Sharpness Point at full speed and approximately 300 yards from shore an enormous sea hit the lifeboat before the vessel could be brought head on. The *Richard Silver Oliver*, which was not a self-righting lifeboat, was thrown over on to her side and drifted into shore.

Of the ten on board only four survived. The bowman Jacob Brunton was thrown clear and struggled ashore almost unconscious. John William Smith, the District Engineer, and the two lifeboat men, Andrew Tweedy and James Carmichael, were all trapped under the lifeboat. Smith managed to get to the stern of the boat and after being washed off the boat a number of times struck for the shore and somehow to safety. Tweedy who had been trapped by ropes around his leg managed to get himself free and clung to the overturned boat where Carmichael joined him. They both clung to the boat until she was washed ashore.

The lifeboat came ashore in King Edward's Bay, Tynemouth, together with the six dead bodies. It was still not 3.30 in the afternoon and this tragedy and dreadful loss of life had taken less than ninety minutes to play itself out.

On 24th April 1939 the *Richard Silver Oliver* returned under her own power to Cullercoats Lifeboat Station. The tragedy left behind three widows and five children under the age of sixteen years.
Understandably the Cullercoats lifeboat men no longer wished to crew the ill-fated lifeboat and the *Westmorland* replaced the *Richard Silver Oliver* in February 1940.

The ill fated *Richard Silver Oliver*.

Cullercoats did not escape wartime casualties, although, it fared better than some of the surrounding towns and the city of Newcastle. On 6th May 1941 bombs dropped from a German aircraft killed three people in Garden Square, Cullercoats.

On 8th August 1942 a German bomber in a hit and run raid attacked the village. John Street Methodist Church was destroyed and a 13-year-old local boy, who was inside the church practising on the organ, was killed instantly. Bombs also landed on the railway line just south of Cullercoats Station, on Marden Avenue and on Kenners Dene Farm, Tynemouth.

The imposing John's Street Methodist Church before it was destroyed by a German bomber in 1942.

The church, after it was bombed, where a 13-year-old boy was killed whilst he was practising the organ.

The worst tragedy of the war to affect the village happened during a night raid on 11th and 12th October 1942. Seven houses in St George's Road and the surrounding area were destroyed and a further ten damaged. Six local people were killed and another seventeen severely injured.

SS *Zephyros* was a Greek steamer of advancing years. Built in 1908 on the Clyde and registered as a 4,796-ton ship, she was originally called the *Dunedin*. At 6 am on 26th February 1947 she was lying at anchor off the Tyne in one of the worst snow blizzards seen for many a year when her anchor chain parted. The vessel had sailed from Rouen the previous Sunday and was awaiting entry into the Tyne for repairs. Within half an hour the ship drove ashore at Brown's Point, ships' hooters sounding continuously and was left high and dry. The crew of 35 men walked ashore when the tide receded having refused to be rescued by the breeches buoy.

Wrecked ships have always been fair game for plundering but only after the crew is rescued and accounted for. The *Zephyros* was a magnet to the local population. It was said that as quick as the crew were abandoning ship others were boarding the ship for the spoils.

On Sunday 9th March 1947 Gunner Bernard Joseph Connolly, a married man from Liverpool and Gunner Percival, who were both stationed at Tynemouth Castle, unlawfully boarded the abandoned vessel. Connelly tragically fell into the hold of the ship and was drowned.

The *Zephyros*, high and dry on the rocks at Brown's Point, where she remained as a landmark for many years until she was finally broken up for scrap.

On 2nd April 1947 four local men appeared on separate charges of theft before Whitley Bay Magistrates Court where a story of wholesale pillaging was related. The 'spoils' amounted to a gramophone, a roll of sailcloth, a bottle of wine, numerous lamps and tins of paint. The defendants all pleaded guilty and were fined as follows: Arthur Dickinson of 44 Hudleston Street, Cullercoats, fined £3; William Scott of Hudleston Street, Cullercoats, fined £1; James Bailey of Station Road and William Reed of Elizabeth Street, Cullercoats, fined £1.

Sixteen days later 8 juveniles aged between 10 years and 15 years were fined for plundering the *Zephyros*.

The *Zephyros* was to remain a landmark in Brown's Bay for many years where she lay derelict. In 1948 plans were put in place to refloat the remaining hull of the vessel and tow it into the Tyne but the plans came to nought. One final attempt was made in 1951 but this too failed. The *Zephyros* was scrapped where she came ashore.

The 30th May 1950 was another tragic day for the lifeboat at Cullercoats. Renowned and revered as a lifeboat station which had saved many lives, the lifeboat killed a shore helper when she returned from an engine trial run. At this time the lifeboat was physically manhandled back up the beach by upwards of twenty men but by a tragic accident this well rehearsed and oft repeated process caused the death of Thomas Stewart, 66 years, of Simpson Street, Cullercoats. The lifeboat had been placed on the carriage but when the winch wire was slackened the lifeboat slipped back and slid off the carriage trapping Stewart by the legs. Despite prompt medical attention and the amputation of his legs Stewart succumbed to his injuries.

Douglas (Dougie) Clark is still a fisherman at the age of 79 years but in May 1948, whilst fishing alone in his coble the *Jenny* half a mile offshore, he flirted with an early death at the age of 25 years. His wooden coble caught fire and the fire quickly took a hold. Fortunately a number of fishermen saw the smoke from the fire and set off to rescue Dougie. Apparently when the rescuers got alongside the *Jenny*, Dougie appeared quite unperturbed, although, he had taken the precaution of constructing a makeshift life raft and had divested himself of his sea boots. Dougie and his coble, smoke and flames billowing from her bow, were taken into Cullercoats Bay where the boat was scuttled and quickly sank in the shallow waters, which put out the flames. The cause of the fire was due to a backfire from the engine that ignited some petrol.

If any reader has ever travelled to the USA, one of the questions on the visa waiver form asks if the applicant has ever been involved in espionage. This always strikes me as an absurd question as I am sure spies would have the skills to evade this question but for one Cullercoats-born person if he answered correctly I am sure the Immigration Authorities would refuse him entry.

On 19th November 1954 the *Whitley Seaside Chronicle* headlined this story. 'Cullercoats Man Charged under Official Secrets Act.' John Clarence, who at this time was 27 years of age, was a son of Cullercoats who apparently sold the details of the anti-aircraft defences in the North East to the Russians. Clarence was convicted of the charges just before Christmas 1954 and sentenced to 5 years imprisonment.

Cullercoats may only be just over 300 years old as a settlement but obviously very much older feet had crossed the area. In March 1955 Tommy Brown of Cullercoats found a Roman coin beside the sea wall by the lifeboat station. The bust on the coin showed Emperor Hadrian and the coin was dated AD 134. It is believed that the coin had been struck to commemorate the building of the Roman Wall.

Front Street looking north with the Fishermen's Mission at the end of the street.

The quaintness and charm of Cullercoats' traditions and heritage meant little to the local council when, from 1957, they announced one plan after another for the benefit of Cullercoats. Regardless of what plan was put forward, scant regard appeared to be paid to the history of the village. The Cullercoats fishwife was to be eradicated with the demolition of Browns Buildings, the last of the fishermen's cottages. The march of progress was relentless and the history of the village for the next two decades was consumed with demolition, redevelopment and compulsory purchase of property to the dismay of the majority of the residents.

On 26th July 1957 the *Whitley Seaside Chronicle* quoted a Tynemouth official as saying, 'There is no cause for alarm in Cullercoats on the part of those people who may be affected by these redevelopment plans. Redevelopment will only take place as and when the land is available.' What the official failed to mention was that the use of compulsory purchase of property would free up the land.

In 1967 Tynemouth Corporation announced that it was to buy a large part of Cullercoats by compulsory purchase. By now eight different schemes had been proposed and then discarded. The planners and redevelopers tore out the heart of Cullercoats and left an empty unrecognisable shell. Cullercoats as it was then was to be demolished and the only remaining buildings that they proposed would be left standing was to be the Bay Hotel and the Newcastle Arms. They did not even get this right.

Simpson Street on a snowy winter's day before demolition. Only one side of the street remains.

Simpson Street is now a row of twenty-five cottages, which if the planners had had their way in 1973, would have been demolished under compulsory purchase. The cottages are the one surviving link with the fishing industry of the past. Fortunately Central Government thwarted the plans for demolition and the cottages were upgraded and modernised.

However, for tenants on the opposite side of the road eight families received a nasty shock from the Electricity Board when they found that the board had put out their Christmas tree lights just before Christmas 1975. Their houses were scheduled for demolition at the turn of the year and the ever-efficient Electricity Board had disconnected the electricity. Apparently Tynemouth Council had omitted to tell the residents that their houses were to be demolished. A spokesman for the council was quoted as saying, 'There seems to have been a misunderstanding here and we are not sure how it has arisen.' Quite an understatement.

Today one side of Simpson Street remains and shows what could have done to those fishermen's cottages, which were demolished.

On 3rd August 1973 the *Whitley Bay Guardian* carried the headline, 'Is council trying to destroy Cullercoats?' A prospective Liberal candidate for Tynemouth echoed the thoughts of many residents when he said, 'It is hard to distinguish whether Tynemouth Council are planning the redevelopment or the destruction of Cullercoats. There seems to have been no research into the social and personal aspects of redeveloping the village.' By now a residents' action committee had been formed but whilst they were trying to have an input in the redevelopment plans compulsory notices for the purchase for much of their property were already being served.

The uniqueness of Cullercoats appeared to count for little. Cullercoats at the time was something rare – a real community. The people were all tied together through friends and relations who lived close by. Results of a survey showed that of the 387 people living in the redevelopment area covering 160 houses only 15 of them were prepared to leave the village. Forty-nine of the houses were owner-occupied and every one of them was prepared to improve their houses with the assistance of improvement grants. Of the 387 villagers affected 107 had relatives within the village.

'We are only here for the tears,' was the lament of the regulars of the Newcastle Arms when it was learnt that Tynemouth Council had reneged on earlier promises and decided that the old public house was to be demolished in September 1973. The pub in Front Street was built in 1815 and was one of the four great pubs of the fishing era. The demolition was to make way for a car park for the nearby Bay Hotel. One of the regulars is quoted in the *Whitley Bay Guardian* as saying, 'Big business is ripping Cullercoats apart.' The owners of the pub, Scottish and Newcastle Breweries, were opposed to the plan but were forced to capitulate in the face of a compulsory purchase order. It would appear that car parking was considered more important than people.

The Newcastle Arms called last orders on 26th September 1973 when the patrons staged a mock funeral. A coffin and a wreath were placed on the bar and a funeral oration was read. Another landmark and piece of Cullercoats history was reduced to rubble within a few weeks.

Protestations continued from residents regarding the demolition of their houses but to no avail. Sparrow Hall, built in 1681, was reduced to rubble in 1979.

When the old fishermen's cottages on the seafront at Cullercoats were demolished many people thought that the character of the village would disappear. In some ways they were right but the bay remains unscathed and so do the memories of the old cottages and the style of life they personified. This chronicle now comes to an end. The infrastructure of the village may have been for many, myself included, inextricably damaged with a thoughtless and ill-considered redevelopment but it still remains Cullercoats Village with a community spirit bar none.

Images of old Cullercoats

Janice Jefferson, later to become McCully, Robert and John Jefferson at the back of Simpson Street.

Front Street looking south with the Watch Tower in the distance.

FISHWIVES

The Cullercoats fishwives were proud
people and fortunately were not camera
shy. This is Kitty Donkin in her best clothes
posing for a studio shot.

The Cullercoats fisherfolk of the nineteenth and twentieth century were very clannish and generally intermarried amongst themselves. There was sound economic sense for this arrangement. The young men of the village had no reason to go outside the community for a wife who was also his helpmate. The work done by his wife was hard, arduous and needed special skills. The baiting of the lines was a delicate and subtle operation, whilst the business of seeking bait, needed local knowledge. A Cullercoats girl was used to being barefoot and enduring the cold of the North Sea. Marrying outside of the village was seen as wrecking his life chances and the gossips were quick to tell him of that. A stranger would also have difficulty in being accepted.

A letter printed in the *Port of Tyne Pilot* dated 8th June 1839 from an anonymous writer attested, 'it has long been a custom followed from time immemorial for the lasses of Cullercoats to mate with none but the lads of their own village – fishermen, who at least, could never turn up their noses at garments redolent of fish. Their courtships were quiet and uninterrupted. As soon as a girl found herself able to maintain a house, she accepted the hand of the lad who had from her infancy lessened her daily toil and cheered her leisure hours.' Most girls of the village had married and were mothers by the age of 16 years.

In the 1830s a gentlemen describing Cullercoats said that it was becoming famous as a residence of famous artists who found the beauties of the surroundings together with the noble type of fishermen and the fine models of the female beauty among the fisher-lasses good subjects for their pictures. Even past middle age these hardy women carried themselves with a gracefulness which was the envy of the their sisters in the nearby towns. Their stout hearts and strength of character belied the strong bond and sympathetic feelings for others in their village.

In 1882 Aaron Watson, a journalist and President of the South Shields Art Club, described the Cullercoats fishwife in the following terms: 'The women are the working bees. Stout, hardy creatures, with petticoats of blue flannel, and such common agreement in their style of dress as to seem as if they wore a uniform; they stand on the beach in the morning fully equipped for a hasty journey to town … In Cullercoats everything is primitive. As a fishing station, Shields is going through a rapid progress of development; but, though it is only two miles away, Cullercoats has been untouched by the waves of change.'

The rhythm of life for the fishwives and the fishermen was determined by the sailing boats setting out at dark and returning in the early morning. When the boats returned from fishing the division of labour was time honoured. The men handed the catch over the side and then went home to bed. The fishwives shared out the catch, filled the creels that went on their backs and set out as far a field as Newcastle, Spennymoor and Blyth selling their wares calling out in shrill and musical tones 'Buy fee-s-ch.'

They were trained from childhood to shoulder the creels upon their backs. Small ones for the children, gradually increasing in size and weight, as they grew older and stronger. This was no nine to five, five day a week job. Everyday was a working day.

Annie Smith outside 27 Front Street. The flowers and the photographs are a shrine to her son Thomas, who was killed in the Great War.

Annie Smith's son, Thomas Smith, lost in action on 28th April 1918 at Salonika whilst serving as a private with the Royal Horse Artillery and Royal Field Artillery.

Their ever-watchful eye on the treacherous coast that ran by their doors was always vigilant. They assisted in bringing helpless shipwrecked men ashore and giving them succour and comfort and nursed many back to life. This tradition of service carried through until their demise in the 1960s.

After the Scottish fleets of fishing boats decimated the shoals of fish as they migrated around the coast the Cullercoats men came to depend more heavily on salmon fishing which, by an Act of Parliament, they were allowed to do between 1st February and 31st August each year. For this the fishermen had to take out a licence, the right of which was handed down from father to son. Crabs and lobsters were also potted as a means of supplementing their meagre income.

The move from white fishing to salmon once again changed the rhythm of village life. Cullercoats fishwives travelled to the nearby North Shields Fish Market where they would buy their white fish from commercial outlets, which they would then sell.

Annie Nannie Dick in pensive mood.

Fishwives on North Shields Fish Quay loading their creels for the day's sale.

Once the fish was bought and sorted, the heads were cut off and the fish packed into the creels in alternate directions in order to maximise the number of fish that could be carried. Then they set off with as much as they could carry in their creels, which left permanent marks on their shoulders and their arms. In these days the railway network was much larger and spread widely across the region and Cullercoats fishwives could be seen selling fish in all the suburbs of Newcastle, along the Tyne Valley in Hexham, Stocksfield and even Allenheads. Others went out into the colliery areas of County Durham. For the fishwives their markets radiated out of Cullercoats for up to forty miles.

The longevity of the inhabitants was legendary, which was even more remarkable when life expectancy was compared with the inhabitants of nearby North Shields. This longevity was attributed to keeping the doors and windows open and by living so much in the open air. In the first half of the nineteenth century six people lived to be over one hundred years old and another fifteen lived into their late eighties and nineties.

Perhaps their diet also helped. After the glut of herring landed between July and September their reliance for produce of the sea could not be guaranteed. The plentiful herrings were 'laid' or salted down as they provided the life-blood of subsistence until the following March. This reliance could be summed by an old wit who remarked, 'One day we have herrings and spuds, next day we have spuds and herrings.'

Cullercoats people also developed a vocabulary of their own which was foreign to anyone outside of the village. Grandparents were universally known as 'ganny' and 'gaffy.' Other popular names were:

Stocker	A fish other than a salmon caught in a net
Kneef	A fist
Gully	A bread knife
Puddick	A frog
The retley's	In a minute
Soomin	Swimming
Nammie	A large turnip

Bessie Taylor in 1926 aged 82 years, still active and working selling fish.

Elizabeth Storey (née Taylor) who was known by everyone as Lizzie Butcher, her mother's maiden name.

The Cullercoats fishwives had an instantly recognisable distinct and unique style of dress, which they wore almost as a uniform by the mid-nineteenth century. The Cullercoats outfit consisted of a short jacket similar to a bed gown, which covered the top half of the body, over which they always wore a shawl. The shawl was plain, in grey or black wool, with a fringe and was worn crossed over at the front. The rear point was tucked into the waistband.

The skirt was worn just above the ankle or up to mid-calf length, which allowed for the wearer to wade into the sea without getting the skirt wet. It was tied around the waist with tapes at the back of the skirt. A number of layers were worn for insulation and warmth, which gave a voluminous appearance. An apron worn on top of the skirt completed the outfit.

The younger fishwives tended to go bareheaded, as most of the photographs show, but as they grew older they would wear either a shawl or a traditional straw bonnet. Most fishwives would own two or three sets of working clothes that they would wash daily and a finer set of clothes in the same fashion for high days and special occasions.

The traditional fishermen's cottages, which were such a feature of the village, were very tiny, some of them with just one room where all the family lived, ate and slept. The cottages had stone flag floors covered with either linoleum, sailcloth or a 'clippie mat' made from

Young Sally and Bertha Lisle, from one of the
original Cullercoats families.

torn up blankets or coats. A large bed would dominate the room in one
corner alongside a basic table and chairs with perhaps one easy chair
with a few ornaments to decorate the coal range on which all of the
cooking was done. Toilet facilities were rudimentary and for the most
was outside across the back lane.

The Cullercoats fishwife was incredibly house proud and as most of
their time was spent outdoors the outside of their cottage was kept as
clean as the inside.

In what spare time they had, the fishwives would sit out in the back
lane on their stools, smoking their clay pipes and knitting jerseys and
socks for their men folk. All the fishing communities on the North East
coast knitted a similar type of jersey or 'gansy' with blue wool in a
traditional four needle circular method. Each jersey incorporated a

David and Lizzie Taylor outside their cottage in Browns Buildings.

Lizzie Taylor, Lizzie Lisle and David Taylor outside their cottage.

unique emblem peculiar to that village, which ensured that should any fishermen be drowned and later given up by the sea in such a state that his identity could not be determined, then his jersey would indicate from which village he was from.

Despite this hard life most of the Cullercoats fishwives bore many children. If a fishwife had a small baby then the baby was left at home with an older village woman who minded babies for a shilling a day. The older children looked after the toddlers and older infants, whilst the mother hawked the fish and the father either fished or slept ready for the next fishing trip. Once home there was housework to be done, food to be cooked and the eternal baiting of the lines before making bread for the following day.

Cullercoats fishwives in their finest clothes on Lifeboat Fete Day.

Many years ago in the time of the Musical Halls, Ned Corven a comic singer, joined the Billy Purves Company who were playing at the New Quay, North Shields. He was so impressed with the Cullercoats fishwives that he dedicated one of his compositions to them.

The Cullercoats Fish Lass

Aa's Cullercoats fish-lass, se rosy an' free
Browt up in a cottage just close to the sea
An' aa sell fine fresh fish, both to poor an' te rich
Will you buy, will you buy will you buy ma fresh fish.

Byeth barefut and barelegged aa trudge mony a week
Wi a creel on me back an' a bloom on me cheek
Aa'll supply yee wi' flat fish, fine skyet or fresh ling
And sometimes penny wilks, crabs and lobsters an' bring

Aa work hard for me living, fra a friend a never begs
An' aa huff the young gents as they peep at me legs
Aa's hilthy an' handsome, quite willing and strang
Te toil for me living, crying fish the day lang.

The romance of Nanny Purvis is an old Cullercoats story and whether there is any truth in the story I will leave it to the reader to decide. However, there is much in the story that runs very close to real events.

'Nanny Purvis was often seen baiting her crab baskets or seated by her cottage door mending nets for her sturdy grandchildren. In 1911 all Cullercoats knew her as she knew all Cullercoats for she had grown up to womanhood and loveliness within the village but now age had overtaken her. None acquainted with her in 1911 associated the beauty and grace that she once had with the bent and tanned features of the old woman yet there were those who knew her when she was the pride of the village and young fishermen vied to win her affections.

'Nanny Purvis had her own romance too, a story of a handsome stranger and a simple village maiden. This romance had occurred in 1831 when Cullercoats was not what it was in 1911. The steam locomotive and the wireless telegraph had not brought the village in touch with the outside world. Even the great coaly city of Newcastle was an unknown land to many of its inhabitants and a visitor, who came from farther a field, was a source of great wonderment.

'In the early 1830s Henry Clouston, an artist, the forerunner for many artists, arrived in Cullercoats from London. It was said that he had even lived in Paris. It is no wonder that when he came to sketch their homely cottages and colourful cobles, to loll in the pretty bay and chat with the people, he stirred the sleepy village to its depths. It is no wonder that the local woman fell for his charms as he was rich and handsome and could speak of matters strange and wonderful. Nanny and he became firm friends. Through the summer he stayed on and through into the autumn and then into the winter.

'It was inevitable perhaps that the gossips should talk and ill natured stories concerning Nanny's dealings with 'that artist chap' should make themselves heard and it was inevitable that these stories should come to the hears of Tom Purvis, one of Nanny's favourite suitors. Tom had been the envy of the young men before the arrival of Clouston, but the continuing stories raised him to anger and a conversation one day with one of his male friends sent him into a rage. Jealously has never paused to reason or inquire. Tom was full of outrage and strode into the village. Nanny was busy with some household task and Clouston was in her company. Tom saw the light in Nanny's eyes as she spoke to Clouston and this further enraged him. The sight fuelled the flames of jealousy. He reasoned that the story of the gossips was true. He would have nothing more to do with her.

'Tom Purvis set sail for the fishing that night in bad weather and with the sea breaking over the Piers. No sane fishermen would set sail that night but Tom Purvis was not acting rationally.

'The wind howled and the seas became mountainous as Nanny gathered bait on the rocks occasionally looking out to seaward.

Nellie Wakinshaw, Margaret Dick and Annie Dodds.

Clouston joined her. He spoke fondly to her and took her hand. The moment had arrived that Nanny was expecting. She was promised to Tom Purvis but Clouston had other ideas. He started to talk in a way that was going to lead to a proposal when in the distance Nanny saw the lights of a coble making for the bay. It was Tom Purvis's boat running before the gale. The danger was apparent; Nanny knew the sea and all its moods of calm and storm. The sea was in an ugly mood and the danger to the boat of Tom Purvis was all too apparent.

Lizzie Coxon poses for a family photograph in a studio.

'They rushed down on to the beach and the village assembled to wish the boat, with its crew of two, home safely. The coble bucked and fought its way through the breakers and just as it seemed that she was going to reach the sanctuary of calm waters the coble capsized and threw the crew into the foaming waters.

'For a moment Clouston hesitated and then he saw two figures clinging to the upturned boat. "I'll save him," whispered Clouston to Nanny and disappeared into the sea. Nanny cannot remember the details of the rescue but was told that 'the artist chap' had swum out to the upturned boat with a rope and that Clouston and the two men were dragged back ashore more dead than alive. The hardy fishermen quickly recovered but for Clouston it was otherwise. He grew gradually weaker and weaker and just before he died he looked at Nanny and whispered, "It is alright now Nanny."

'Henry Clouston was buried in the churchyard in Cullercoats. A handsome monument to his memory was erected. But his memorial is enshrined in the recollections of the humble fisherfolk; and his memory was treasured by none other than Tom Purvis's wife, Nanny, who went on to declare when the tale of some erring girl and a handsome lover was retailed by the village gossips that not all gentlemen were rogues and not all village maidens frail.'

Kitty Laidler née Storey.

Elsie Stephenson, *circa* 1903.

There is no doubt that Polly Donkin, who was born in 1857 in Middlesbrough, epitomised the real Cullercoats fishwife. She was born Mary Ann Shuttleworth yet from childhood her mother had called her Polly, though no reason was ever given for this childhood name.

In 1878 John Walker Donkin brought his young wife Polly to live in Simpson's Yard, Cullercoats. The marriage nearly did not take place as they were to be married in Howard Street Methodist Church, North Shields, but on the day of the wedding there had been several days of snowstorms. There were deep drifts between Cullercoats and North Shields and there was only one horse to pull the cab. Another horse was quickly found and the team succeeded in pulling the couple to their marriage and then returning them to Cullercoats as man and wife. Polly later recalled at her Diamond Wedding in her local Northumbrian accent, 'It was a varry stormy night but we have had plenty of sunshine since then.'

John Walker Donkin came from hardy Cullercoats stock, was born in the village and spent all his life there. He was only nine years old when of necessity he began to make his livelihood from the sea and for over 50 years he sailed his coble out of Cullercoats Haven with the salmon fishermen.

Throughout her married life Polly always wore her fishwife's costume – a full-skirted black gown with embroidered bodice and apron. She took to the fisher dress after she was married and stuck to it. As a fishwife Polly roamed far and wide selling her fish. Polly carried her creel laden with fish for 61 years until she was 78 years old.

John and Polly Donkin in the year of their marriage, 1878.

She could be found anywhere from Newcastle to Shotley Bridge, High Spennymoor, Lintz Green and Burnopfield. It was on such a trip whilst she was walking between Friarside and Lintz Green in Durham that two men attacked her and robbed of her day's takings. Her assailants were never caught but Polly was made of sterner stuff and continued to carry on her trade.

In 1930 Polly Donkin was awarded the Gold Brooch by the Royal National Lifeboat Institution in recognition of her services to the lifeboat cause, in particular as a collector of donations. The Cullercoats fishwives commenced collecting for the lifeboat and by 1930 had raised £1,055. Polly was one of the most successful collectors and never failed to beat her record of the previous year. In 1922 she started with £4 and in 1930 at the age of 73 years she collected £57.

The Prince of Wales presented the Gold Brooch to Polly Donkin in London

John Walker Donkin, the love of her life, died at the age of 87 years in April 1946. Five years later Polly joined him when she died in March 1951 aged 93 years.

Polly Donkin through the years

By 1952 there remained only 12 Cullercoats fishwives keeping the tradition and few of them were still hawking their wares. Fiercely independent they continued to cling to their customs. One face, which was well known, was that of Alice Storey who was well known to summer visitors as she sold her crabs and lobsters from her white fronted cottage in Front Street, Cullercoats. Alice had up until two years previous carried her creel with eight to ten stones of fish on her back. Alice was married to Bob Storey, who had been fishing since the age of 12 years, and who was the youngest of seven sons. All his brothers were fishermen.

In 1957 much of the traditions and the heritage of Cullercoats was to be cast aside in the name of progress and development. The local council in their wisdom decided to demolish much of Cullercoats including the fishermen's cottages on the grounds that the properties were unfit to live in or were in a dangerous condition. Alice Storey was now 73 years of age and her husband 83 years old. She declared, 'If they move us away now it will break our hearts.' Other residents made it clear that they wanted to see their lives out in the cottages in which they were born.

Alice and Sally Storey with Bella Mattison.

In 1959 Alice Storey and her elderly husband were forced out of their cottage by an order issued by Tynemouth Council. Alice refused to knuckle under the order. At the Whitsuntide weekend in 1959 she set up her business across the road from the cottage she loved. 'It is heart-breaking watching the old cottages being pulled down. We fishwives were known the world over. Cullercoats will never be the same without the fishwives and the cottages. We never wanted to live anywhere else – but we had to go.' Poetic words.

The second recipient of a Gold Brooch by the Royal National Lifeboat Institution in recognition of her services to the lifeboat cause, in particular as a collector of donations, was awarded to Nannie Lisle. She received the Brooch four days after the disaster that overtook the sinking of the lifeboat, the *Richard Silver Oliver*.

The third Gold Brooch to be awarded to a Cullercoats fishwife was awarded on 15th May 1962 to Isabella (Bella) Maud Mattison of 90 Links Road, Cullercoats. Bella Mattison, although originally a native of North Shields, had lived at Cullercoats for fifty years at the time of receiving her award.

Bella followed in Polly Donkin's footsteps when she became the second fishwife to be presented to a reigning monarch, on 29th October 1954. By this time Bella was known as the 'lifeboat lady' for her tireless collection efforts. In a thirty-two year period Bella collected £3,400.

Fishwives, *circa* 1910.

In June 1963 Bella Mattison received further recognition of her work when she was awarded a BEM in the Queen's Birthday Honours List. Now 84 years of age she was credited with collecting over £6,000 for the lifeboat station. Collecting for the lifeboat by the Cullercoats fishwives had begun in 1922 when Bella was a founder member but by now she was the last remaining fishwife.

The march of progress is unrelenting and it was only a matter of time before the Cullercoats fishwife would become an anachronism. New legislation was being enacted, which they could not adhere to if they continued in their time-honoured ways and the law was unrelenting. The Cullercoats fishwife was by now feeling the weight of the law against them.

On Friday 2nd June 1943 Ellen Stocks, of Simpson Street, Cullercoats, and Jane Alice Tanbin of John Street, Cullercoats, appeared before Newcastle Magistrates Court charged with selling crabs in excess

Janet McCully selling crabs from her
Cullercoats stall.

Bella Jefferson and Janet McCully prepare the crabs for the day.

of the controlled price. They both pleaded guilty and cited ignorance of the law. Both were fined 10 shillings (50p).

On Tuesday 17th August 1943 Cathleen Blake of North View, Cullercoats, appeared before Newcastle Magistrates Court for selling crabs in excess of the controlled price. The magistrates fined her £2 and advised her to carry some scales.

On Tuesday 7th September 1943 Annie Brunton of Front Street, Cullercoats, appeared before Tynemouth Magistrates Court charged with three offences relating to the sale of crabs from her stall outside her house. The summons alleged that she had sold crabs in excess of the controlled price, that she had failed to correctly describe by way of notice what she was selling and that she had failed to keep adequate records. She pleaded guilty and cited ignorance of the law as mitigation for two of the offences. The Chairman of the Magistrates was very sympathetic and said, 'The bench is very sorry to see the defendant here. It is her first offence. It is a very difficult matter to carry some of the regulations out but the regulations are there and they have to be obeyed.' She was fined a total of twenty-five shillings (£1.25p) and given one month to pay. A further three Cullercoats fishwives appeared at court the same day on similar offences and received the same fines.

On 11th January 1946 Elizabeth Downie of Front Street, Cullercoats, appeared before Whitley Bay Magistrates Court charged with selling fish without weighing them. It must have been her unlucky day as her customer was an off duty policewoman. Elizabeth was found guilty and fined forty shillings (£2).

The Cullercoats fishwives and their quaint cottages have been consigned to the history books and the memories of their loved ones. Surely no such small group of people have made such an impact, become part of North East folklore and been so affectionately regarded throughout the area.

Betty Scott outside her cottage, *circa* 1900.

FISHERMEN

Robert Storey at the age of 88 years in 1935 still mending nets.

The original fisher families in the village were the Lisles, Bruntons, Storeys, Armstrongs and Taylors. It was no doubt because of this fact that the same surnames were so prolific that the use of nicknames became so prevalent, some of which seem very longwinded and others mysterious. Nicknames were given early in life and stayed with a person until death.

In 1861 a list of names that manned the lifeboat was printed and many contained the nickname of the individual. Here are some of them:

John Chisholm	*Jack the Devil*	John Smith	*Sailor*
Robert Storey	*Frank's son*	William Dodds	*Honour*
Francis Storey	*Shaw*	Joseph Robinson	*Prince*
William Storey	*Little Bill's son*	Barry Taylor	*Pincher*
Robert Taylor	*Son of Barry*		

Other lifeboat crew and fishermen nicknames have been discovered. They have been written as they were found:

George Lisle	*Geordie AAH*	William Taylor	*Long Billy*
J. Lisle	*Fidler*	J. Taylor	*Ricey*
R. Lisle	*Puddin*	P. Taylor	*Pick*
Andrew Taylor	*Dolly*	J. Lisle	*Little Jackie*
B. Taylor	*Kenny*	George Lisle	*Lepter*
A. Taylor	*Cuddy*	George Scott	*Nasher*
W. Scott	*Billy the Knave*	J. Scott	*Pigeon*
R. Scott	*Bob the Beef*	J. Taylor	*Hair*
J. Taylor	*Unkley*	Joe Taylor	*Memmer*
G. Lisle	*Black Geordie*	J. Taylor	*Willick*
R. Taylor	*Moucher*	Abe Storey	*Little Abe*
John Dick	*Gaffy John*	R. Jefferson	*Little Bobby*
P. Armstrong	*Pie*	J. Harrison	*Mussel Man*
Robert Storey	*Chucky*	R. Laidler	*Dickie Nosh*
J. Armstrong	*Curran*	B. Taylor	*Pick*
R. Taylor	*Mousher*	W. Dodds	*Honour*
G.H. Taylor	*Whistler*	G.H. Taylor	*Gannet*
G. Brunton	*Lepter*	J. Pearson	*Gully*
J. Scott	*Gaffer*	A. Storey	*Little Andy*
H. Brown	*Harry the Buck*	Harry Taylor	*Chapel*
J. Smith	*Sailor*	J. Taylor	*Jimmy Hair*
T. Taylor	*Stocks*	George Brunton	*Roach*
Joe Taylor	*Memmir*	W. Harrison	*Brannen*
George W. Lisle	*Lang Wylli*	C. Lisle	*Big Col*
G. Lisle	*Black Geordie*	J. Brunton	*Gaffy Jake*
J. Lisle	*Tiddler*	J. Carr	*Big Carr*
R. Taylor	*Nashy*	Robert Taylor	*Bobbler*

Mending nets on the boat field on the cliff top. Nearest is believed to be Charlie Taylor with his father, Old Bob, in the bowler hat.

There was little time for leisure and amusement. Most of their leisure time was spent lounging over the railings looking into the bay discussing the way ships were entering and leaving the Tyne or chatting to visitors.

Cullercoats fishermen were initially chiefly dependant upon herring and white fishing, which was principally carried on from July to March. At this time the most profitable branch of the industry was herring fishing. Huge catches in modern day terms were not unusual and it was not uncommon for a single boat to land in excess of 19,000 herring in a single trip.

On 25th August 1840 one boat caught 16,000 herring and was obliged to give up three nets to some other boats. The take was so great that the herring were hawked through the streets of Newcastle by the fishwives at 6 herring for one old penny ($^1/_2$ p). Herring were being sold at a price of 2 shillings and sixpence (12.5p) per thousand.

The life of a Cullercoats fisherman was one of toil and danger. His earnings were rarely large yet his outlay was considerable. The wariness of the salmon meant that a drift net lasted only one season and the cost of bait was a further expense. Initially the fishermen caught their own bait from the extensive mussel beds at the mouth of the Tyne but the dredging operation to make the Tyne a safer harbour destroyed the beds.

The dangers of fishing are well documented and the residents of Cullercoats were no strangers to such tragedies. Their heritage is firmly anchored in the sea but a fisherman's battle with nature is dominated with adherence to superstition. All seafarers are superstitious but there is none more superstitious than the Cullercoats fisherman.

On the day of sailing fishermen, once they had left home, would not look back or turn back. Meeting a clergyman, a funeral cortége or a nun on the way to the boat spelt bad luck. It is reputed that if such an eventuality arose the fisherman would return home and start his journey all over again.

Thomas and John (Lucky, Lucky) Storey.

Their womenfolk were also bound by superstition. They were not allowed to wash clothes on the day of a sailing lest their men 'be washed overboard.' Once he had left home they were not allowed to call after him or go down to the dock to see him off. Whistling was taboo as it might 'whistle up a storm.'

The superstitions continued once at sea. Words such as pig, rabbit, monkey and salmon were never uttered on shore or at sea. Why these words were taboo is lost in the annals of history and folklore. The word pig could not be used but instead grunter or something similar was acceptable. Should any of these taboo words be used by anyone whilst preparing for fishing, then some ill luck would follow such as lost nets or lines or a poor catch. If a stranger inadvertently mentioned such a word the impending ill luck could be averted by, either grasping cold iron, or turning your cap around on your head a full 360 degrees.

CULLERCOATS FISHERMEN MENDING NETS.

Always work to be done whilst discussing the day's catch.

Fishermen's big sea boots were always carried one under each arm with their toes pointing forward. To carry sea boots together with the toes pointing downwards held that the owner would be carried home drowned before the night was over.

In the late nineteenth century a course of ambulance lectures were given in Cullercoats and a skeleton was used to describe the anatomy of the body. A female skeleton was used and it is reported that a large number of fishermen attended the lecture. The next day a terrible storm broke upon the area when many cobles were at sea. The cobles had to run for home and abandon their lines. For this disaster the skeleton was blamed and in deference to their wishes, almost threats, the skeleton was removed from the village. It was never allowed to return. After this incident the attendance figures at the ambulance lectures fell dramatically and were eventually abandoned.

Cobles at rest in the bay after a night's fishing ready for the next trip.

The incessant rhythm of life for a fisherman. Nets mended and stowed. Off in search of a good catch.

The first documented tragedy occurred on 27th November 1772 when the area was hit by a sudden storm after the fishing fleet had set sail in moderate weather. A sudden gale arose with the sea coming on very high. The cobles abandoned their lines and headed for the safety of the bay.

One boat capsized and was lost with the deaths of four local men. The deceased were Thomas Pearson, Andrew Gray and his son, and William Donkin who were all drowned. No record can be found of the name of the coble but it is reported that with some difficulty other boats and their crews landed late in the afternoon in 'a pitiful condition.'

On 17th April 1810 a number of Cullercoats cobles were hauling and re-baiting their lines when they were overcome by a sudden south east gale and driven north of Cullercoats. They were seen off Hartley (now known as Seaton Sluice) and a rescue attempt made by the Blyth lifeboat. The lifeboat had been dragged along the shore to Hartley. Eleven fishermen were taken off their boats into the lifeboat but instead of running for Blyth the lifeboat attempted to beach itself from where it had been launched. The lifeboat was hit by a heavy sea, driven ashore and totally wrecked. Twenty-six or the twenty-eight men on board were drowned. Fifteen lifeboat men from Blyth and Hartley perished together with eleven Cullercoats fishermen. The Cullercoats casualties were William Armstrong and his four sons; James Smith and his three sons; Robert Renner and a young man called Taylor.

On the morning of 1st February 1848 seven local men set sail in a coble to take a pilot to a ship lying off the mouth of the Tyne bound for South Shields. The morning was clear and fine, the seas were running high and the wind squally from the north west. The coble had just cleared the harbour when it was swamped and capsized by a heavy sea off the bay at Cullercoats. The local men drowned within sight of onlookers and their families.

The deceased were George Lisle (57 years), his two sons Robert (24) and George (34), his brother Robert Lisle (50), Robert Clark his brother-in-law, James Stocks and Charles Pearson. Stocks made a gallant struggle for life before he succumbed to his fate and though he was repeatedly washed off the back of the coble he managed to get back to it. However, he was weakening. He stripped off his clothes and prepared to swim ashore watched by his brother who was standing by on the rocks. His brother shouted to him, 'Jim, swim ashore.' But he answered, 'I'm done, I'm done,' and hung his head into the sea and sank.

The sea did not give up the body of the father George Lisle until 18th March 1848 when he was washed up at Tynemouth. Four bodies were never recovered. The graves of those from the same family can be seen in the grounds of Tynemouth Priory. The disaster greatly affected the Duke of Northumberland who owned much of the land in and around Cullercoats. He responded by providing the funds for the establishment of a lifeboat station at Cullercoats. This was one of the worst tragedies to hit the village and is still remembered today. Six women were widowed and fourteen children under the age of eleven years were left fatherless.

In June 1860 the village was in mourning again following the loss of three of its fishermen. Two Cullercoats cobles had left for the fishing grounds in the middle of the day when all was fair. They were overrun by a storm as darkness descended. One of the cobles was towed into North Shields by a Scottish fishing boat with a loss of all gear but the other coble had disappeared. The deceased were William Harrison, George Armstrong and Frank Storey. Two wives lost their husbands and six very young children were left fatherless and at the mercy of charity.

Early morning landing of the catch just as dawn breaks.

More fishermen's lives were lost on Tuesday 25th April 1871 when a coble foundered within sight of the village and the three crewmembers drowned. The coble was fishing for salmon in a heavy swell just off Crab Point, a short distance from Cullercoats, when she was driven ashore. Before the crew could recover themselves she was struck by a heavy wave, which carried the crewmembers into the sea. The drowning of the men was not witnessed by anyone and considerable anxiety arose in the village when the coble became long overdue. A search of the area quickly found the coble upside down on Crab Point. The deceased were Joseph Brunton, John Storey and a boy called Pearson. The body of John Storey was found entangled in the nets of the upturned boat and it is believed that the sea gave up the other bodies shortly afterwards. Two wives and seven young children were left to mourn their passing.

Human nature can sometimes be cruel and exploitative. Following this tragedy it was necessary for Reverend R.F. Wheeler, The Vicarage, Whitley Bay, to write a letter, which was published in the *Shields Daily News* on 3rd May 1871. It warned readers that certain parties were going door to door in North Shields soliciting subscriptions for the deceased's families – which was a fraud.

On Saturday 2nd December 1878 five Cullercoats fishing cobles set sail from the harbour at 8 am to fish for haddock and codling. They were the *Queen of the North* owned by A. Taylor; *Margaret* owned by H. Brown; *The Brothers* owned by W. Dodd; *The Ranger* owned by G. Armstrong and the *George* owned by George Nicholson.

At mid-day heavy rain and a strong east south easterly gale sprang up and the seas turned angry. The Cullercoats lifeboat put to sea to assist any of the cobles should they run for home and try and gain entry into the harbour. Time and again the first four cobles tried to enter the harbour but were beaten back by the dangerous conditions and they made off for the Tyne entrance.

At 2.15 pm that day the *George* was seen trying to run for the bay and the locals who had gathered along the shoreline tried to warn her off by signalling by flag for her to make for the Tyne. Apparently not seeing the flag the *George* attempted to enter Cullercoats Harbour and was immediately capsized as she ran over the harbour bar. The four crewmen were thrown into the boiling seas but fortunately Ephraim Stocks managed to grab hold of an oar. The other three men were seen clinging on to the upturned boat but were swept to their deaths before the lifeboat could rescue them. Ephraim Stocks was saved.

The deceased were named as George Armstrong (22) who left a widow and a young child; Selby Adamson who left a widow and six young children, three girls and three boys and George Nicholson who was single and the son of the owner of the coble.

By the late 1880s Cullercoats, like many other small ports, was under pressure from the rise of the steam trawler. The fishermen began to fish more for haddock, cod, whiting, ling and turbot and between February and August for salmon.

After nearly half a century of immunity from disaster at sea the fishing community at Cullercoats lost three of their number in a storm, which increased in violence after midnight on Wednesday 11th April 1929.

They were James Scott (58), nicknamed Pigeon, his son William Scott (24) and William Taylor (38) who formed the crew of the coble SN 144 *Mary Scott*. All three men resided in Simpson Street, Cullercoats. In the early hours of Thursday morning when it became known that the *Mary Scott* had not returned to port a gloom of sorrow was cast over the village and men and women congregated in groups on the foreshore. At first, news of the fate of the boat and the crew was uncertain, but quickly a rumour spread that the wreckage of the *Mary Scott* had been found off Marsden. The vessel had been pounded to splinters by the incessant waves but there was no sign of the crew.

The *Mary Scott* had been salmon fishing with the Cullercoats coble *Queen Elizabeth*, a Newbiggin coble *Our Girls*, another Cullercoats coble *Nellie Mavis* and two North Shields cobles. The weather gradually worsened with a high running sea and the wind increasing to a gale. With the exception of the *Mary Scott* the other cobles ran for shelter into the Tyne whilst the *Mary Scott* continued to fish.

Poignantly another son of William Scott, Frank, who had been aboard the coble *Queen Elizabeth*, found the wreckage. With the breaking of daylight revealing that the *Mary Scott* had not returned to port, Frank Scott rode down to the Marsden cliffs on his motorcycle where he found the wreckage of the *Mary Scott*. No bodies could be found.

The only body that was recovered was that of the skipper James Scott that the sea gave up a few days after the tragedy near to where the wreckage was found. A local penned the following poem, which was printed in the *Whitley Seaside Chronicle*:

The Mary Scott left Cullercoats with a crew of three
No coble better manned did ever put out to sea
She headed straight for Marsden near to Frenchman's Bay
The mighty ocean fishing ground where fish abound and play

They threw the anchor overboard, straightway shot the net
Settled down to wait the catch amidst the spray and wet
When suddenly a sea sprang up the coble pitched and tossed
Alas the squall upset the boat and three brave men were lost

Cullercoats fisherman Jacob Smith wearing the distinctive blue woollen 'gansy.'

The Cullercoats coble SN 80 *Endeavour* was salmon fishing on Saturday 9th May 1936 when disaster overtook it. The loss of the coble was not witnessed and the alarm not raised until the body of man was found by a River Tyne Police Officer by the North Pier at Tynemouth. Twenty yards away from the body was the wreckage of the coble *Endeavour*. The coble had been torn apart and fears grew that it had been run down. The body was identified as Gilbert Joseph Crawshaw, 29 years, of 80 Hudleston Street, Cullercoats.

The coble should have been manned by three men but the third hand, a man named Simpson, of Links Road, Cullercoats, had arrived at North Shields Fish Quay ten minutes late for the sailing. The coble had gone to sea without him. At this time the owner of the boat Bolam Dick, 33 years, also of Hudleston Street, Cullercoats, was missing.

The body of Bolam Dick was eventually found by divers wedged under a huge rock by the North Pier. They could not extricate him from his watery grave. The crane *Titan* that stood on the North Pier at Tynemouth for many years succeeded after a number of unsuccessful attempts in lifting the boulders off Bolam Dick and his body was released. Both of the deceased men were members of the Cullercoats lifeboat.

A small part of the large fleet of Cullercoats cobles.

The whole village went in mourning for the two fishermen and on the day of the funeral every blind in Hudleston Street was drawn. Flags on the Watch Tower, the Lifeboat House and Dove Marine flew at half-mast. The coffins of both men were brought out of their houses through the windows and in accordance with tradition the coffins made one last circuit of Cullercoats so that the deceased could make 'their final round.' Both men were buried at Preston Cemetery.

The following remembrance was printed in the local newspaper for Selby Adamson following his loss of life on board the *George*.

An Affectionate Remembrance of

SELBY ADAMSON

Who was accidentally drowned off Cullercoats Bar,

ON DECEMBER 2ND, 1876

AGED 34 YEARS

He left his home in perfect health
He little thought of death so nigh
But God thought fit to call him home
And with his will we must comply

Weep not for me my friends so dear
For you I long to see
Your time on earth will not be long
Prepare to follow me

Farewell my wife and children dear
For we on earth will meet no more
But may we all meet around Christ's throne
When time with you all shall be no more

Yes dear wife and children too
God thought fit that I must part from you
Therefore dry up your tears and from sorrow refrain
For God can raise us all up to meet again

Jane and William Taylor, from one of the first established families in Cullercoats.

The graceful lines of a
Cullercoats Coble.

George Lisle, Cullercoats
fisherman and coxswain
of Tynemouth lifeboat
1938-42.

THE UBIQUITOUS COBLE

SN 7 *James Denyer*, owned by Robert Oliver, one of only three cobles left in the village.

The unique coble is indigenous to a 170-mile strip of coastline in the North of England and Southern Scotland. Cobles were designed and developed for particular conditions along this stretch of coastline where there are few safe harbours. Every point of landing is totally different and the presence of the boats and fishing communities gave them strong individual identities.

Although since the industrial revolution several river mouths have been deepened by way of dredging and some new harbours built, such as at Craster, these facilities did not exist in the Norse and Medieval times when the boat was first built. These boats had of necessity to be beach boats, which could be launched and landed, direct on to the beach.

The coble is an ancient form of boat, probably brought to the North East by the Danes who established fishing settlements from the Humber northwards. Much debate has been expounded over the name coble. The name probably comes from the word *cuople*, a much earlier type of boat, which is mentioned in 950 AD by Alfred, a Northumbrian monk, who used the word in the Lindisfarne Gospels. In old Yorkshire from the Tees to the Humber the name is pronounced, 'cobble' whilst further north the word is pronounced with a long 'o' as in cobalt.

The Blyth registered *Three Sisters* currently at North Shields. This coble was the last to be built at Amble in 1986.

Cullercoats cobles were usually built in Hartlepool or Whitby. Few plans exist of cobles as they were built by eye and experience. The coble is an open boat, 27 to 32 feet in length, with a beam of between 6 and 8 feet. They were clinker built, made of larch with a high and bold bow and a square raking stern. The flat bottom allows them to float in 2 inches of water and the tiller is 5 to 6 feet in length that is connected to a large rudder. Prior to the use of motor power the cobles were sail powered with two-master sails, one large and one small. The square sails were dyed with a heavy brown red preservative. Most cobles of the period were painted cobalt blue above the water line with white below. They were crewed by two men and a boy and were mainly family owned and crewed.

The Blyth registered *Gratitude* in Cullercoats boat yard.

Though small in size the coble is very seaworthy but it requires great nerve, skill and experience to manage it. They possess features that give them a distinctive character. Two bilge keels give them some stability and protect the boat's bottom whilst it was being beached. A broad rudder acts like a centreboard when the wind is on the beam and is so fixed to give a great hold on the water. However, if the rudder broke and was lost at sea nothing could save the coble. It would immediately capsize. A good coble grips the sand with her deep bow or forefoot as she is beached which prevents the boat from being washed sideways. When coming ashore towards the beach the deep forefoot would grip the beach and the stern would swing around inshore so that the coble could be beached stern first.

This forefoot, however, made the coble difficult to sail and difficult to row. Whilst in sail, if the vessel was pressed hard, in a sudden wind the deep bow would dig into the water and literally trip the boat up and cause her to roll over. The forefoot also caused problems when being rowed. Depending on the wind direction two men would have to row from one side of the boat with a third man on the other side to keep a coble in a straight line. Early fishermen, before the application of the motor power to a coble, would prefer to row in bad weather and it is by no coincidence that all of the early lifeboats were 'pulling boats' which relied on power by oars. The famous rescue of the passengers from the *Forfarshire* off the Farne Islands by William Darling and his daughter Grace was affected in a coble using only oars for propulsion.

Working the sailing cobles called for total commitment from the whole community. The women would get up early in the morning with the men just as daylight was about to break and would help launch the cobles. The women then returned home to skin the mussels and bait the hooks. They would then return to the shoreline when their men returned home and helped land the boats and unload the catch.

The names given to the Cullercoats cobles varied from the quaint, picturesque to describing good virtues or family relations. In the 1890s the following Cullercoats cobles could be seen in the bay or pulled up on the boat field: *Sea Flower*; *Star of Peace*; *Pilgrim*; *Pride of Cliff*; *Lily of the Valley*; *Swiftsure*; *Quickstep*; *Cock Robin*; *Robin Hood*; *Good Samaritan*; *Good Design*; *Temperance Star*; *Rock of Ages*; *Grand Old Man*; *Confido Deo*; *Amaranth*; *Ancient Promise*; *Welcome Home*; *Village Belle*; *Young William*; *Ripple Gold*; *Shelumiel*; *Moderation*; *Gratitude* and *Amity*.

The square-raking transom of the SN 7 *James Denyer*.

By 1893 over 80 boats were fishing out of Cullercoats. They were all the unique coble. The owners of these boats were also often pilots for the River Tyne, who would search the seas as far south as the Yorkshire coast, hoping to find a ship in need of their services. The coble would then be towed stern first with a fixed rudder to prevent the coble yawing behind the towing ship.

Cullercoats coble, the Blyth registered BH 84 *Crystal River* undergoing maintenance.

Within the next two decades it is likely that the coble will disappear. Today in Cullercoats only 3 cobles remain – the SN 7 *James Denyer*, BH 84 *Crystal River* and BH 452 *Gratitude*.

The ornate nameplate of the *Gratitude*.

The following cobles fished out of Cullercoats Bay between 1860-1960.

Name of Coble	Owner	Name of Coble	Owner
Admiral	A. Dick	Glad Tidings	W. Carr
Alice Taylor	A. Taylor	Gloriana	George Storey
Alpa	N. Fairbairn & son	Golden City	Heddon Taylor
Amity	J. Lisle	Golden Down	Gil Taylor
Anaranth	Abe Storey	Good Samaritan	Chas Taylor
Ann & Sarah	J. Taylor	Grand Old Man	A. Shuttleworth
Annie	George Lisle	Guiding Star	D. Taylor
Annie Dick	John Dick	Hannah Taylor	B. Taylor
Annie Jane	B. Taylor	Harbour Bell	G.H. Taylor
Bessie Carr	W. Carr	Harbour Lights	G.H. Taylor
Bessie Lisle	Joe Lisle	Harold	C. Gascoigne
Brothers	G. Brunton	Harriot & Jane	R. Wilson
Carol	Raymond Oliver	Heavens Gift	Thomas Nicholson
Catherine Laidler	Martin Laidler	Her Majesty	W. Dodds
Childrens Friend	W. Scott	Holy City	G. Storey
Confido Dido	J. Bolam	Honour	W. Dodds
Consolation	R. Scott	Hotspur	J. Donkin
Content	J. Storey	Hugh Gilmore	A. Taylor
Dawn	J. Chisholm	Humility	R. Taylor
Dolly	A. Taylor	Inflexible	George Laidler
Economy	J. Harrison	Indefatigable	G. Lisle
Edward	A. Taylor	Invincible	G. Brunton
Eleanor	J. Scott	Isabella	F. Taylor
Elizabeth	R. Jefferson	Jane Douglas	J. Pearson
Elizabeth Scott	George Scott	Jennet Holmes	J. Scott
Elizabeth Taylor	J. Taylor	John & Kitty	J. Lisle
Elizabeth Taylor	David Taylor	Joseph William	G. Lisle
Ellen	J. Donkin	Joyfull	A. Storey
Endeavour	Bolam Dick	Kitty Storey	R. Storey
England's Glory	P. Armstrong	Kitty Wilson	R. Wilson
Esther	J. Taylor	Lindisfarne	William Taylor
Europe	A. Taylor	Little Hem	Robert Smith
Faithfull	R. Laidler	Lizzie Alver	R. Scott
Fanny Storey	Robert Storey	Lovely Lady	George Brunton
Fisher Lass	F. Taylor	Lydie May	Jack Brunton
Four Brothers	Scott Brothers	Maggie	J. Storey
Fram	Tom Dick	Maggie Storey	W. Storey
Freedom	T. Lisle	Man of Nazareth	G.W. Grant
George & Jane	T. Pearson	Margaret	R. Storey
George & Jane	George Scott	Margaret Armstrong	J. Armstrong
George Retford	J. Armstrong	Mary Ellen	P. Taylor

Name of Coble	Owner	Name of Coble	Owner
Mary Jane	J. Wilson	*Sarah Taylor*	R. Taylor
Mary Scott	J. Scott	*Sea Flower*	R. Storey
May Flower	Harry Taylor	*Sea Quest*	Robert Bell
Millicent	J. Bolam	*Shamrock*	Robert Robson
Miriam	Robert Arthur	*Shelumial*	C. Lisle
Nancy 1	H. Brown	*Silver Spray*	J.H. Taylor
Nancy 2	Robert Hunter	*Sir Wilfred Layson*	Harry Bryson
Nelly Mavis	J. Taylor	*Six 45*	W. Dodds
Newcastle Lass	J. Lisle	*Star Castle*	George Lisle
Non Parell	E. Wilson	*Star Cross*	William Taylor
Old Sea Dog	J. Smith	*Star of Hope*	R. Taylor
Palestine	W. Nicholson	*Starling*	R. Taylor
Perfection	J. Harrison	*Sun Beam*	Harry Bryson
Perseverance	R. Scott	*Tasmania*	P. Armstrong
Pilot Me	William Pearson	*Temperance Star*	W. Scott
Pilot Me	W. Pearson Jnr	*Thistle*	William Taylor
Polly	J. Cole	*Thomasina*	G. Brunton
Primrose	W. Taylor	*Three Brothers*	J. Brunton & Bros
Princess Mary	Joe Taylor	*Thunderer*	J. Brunton
Princess Rose	R. Smith	*True Vine*	A. Scott
Progress	George Brunton	*Tweed*	G. Lisle
Protector	J. Taylor	*Undaunted*	J. Stocks
Providence	T. Taylor	*Unity*	J. Lisle
Providence	J. Stocks	*Universal*	R. Lisle
Provider	Joe Simpson	*Vesta*	Robert Taylor
Queen Elizabeth	J. Scott	*Victoria*	J. Storey
Queen Mary	John Taylor	*W E Gladston*	R. Taylor
Queen of the May	J. Chisholm	*Wilhelmina*	Lisle Smith
Redvers Buller	J. Armstrong	*Windsor Castle*	R. Jefferson
Reliance	J. Brunton	*Windsor Lass*	J. Carr
Rock of Ages	Geo W. Lisle	*Windward Lass*	R.H. Storey
Rock of Safety	Heddon Taylor	*Wings of the Morning*	J. Scott
Rockcliffe	W. Harrison	*Young Ellen*	J. Storey
Rohilla	Robert Smith	*Young George*	G. Scott
Rose	R. Taylor	*Young Jane*	T. Wilson

Mrs Oliver's petrol station, John Street.

Rockcliffe Coachworks, Front Street.

LIFEBOATS AND LIFEBOAT MEN

Robert 'Scraper' Smith, holder of the Lifeboat VC.

No book on Cullercoats would be complete without reference to the Lifeboat Station at Cullercoats. However, this chapter does not seek to be an exhaustive account of the activities over the years of the Cullercoats lifeboat as this has been well documented in other publications.

Tyneside has given the world many inventions, the steam locomotive, the steam turbine and many others but no invention has given greater contribution to humanity than the idea of a boat designed to proceed to sea in any weather to bring help to those in peril when all seems lost. The history of the lifeboat is a local story and is firmly grounded in the counties of Northumberland and Durham, which have produced so many fine ships and accomplished seamen, and which played such a leading part in the origin, growth and development of the lifeboat.

In 1786 a clergyman, Archdeacon Sharp of Northumberland, sent a coble to London coachbuilder Lionel Lukin for modification to make it safer and less likely to sink. The returned boat was never referred to as a lifeboat but was stationed at Bamburgh where she is reputed to have saved many lives in and around the Farne Islands. This was not a purpose-built boat specifically for the rescue of lives but a conversion of a fishing boat.

In 14th March 1789 a Northerly gale was blowing and a flood tide was making life difficult for the fleet of colliers trying to enter the Tyne. Many of them were driven close to the Herd Sands and narrowly missed being wrecked. The Newcastle owned brig *Adventure* was less fortunate. For over twenty-four hours she tried time and again to enter the river mouth in ferocious winds but eventually was driven ashore on the Herd Sands, South Shields. The seas were mountainous and a large group of spectators gathered to watch as the waves pounded the vessels to pieces. Local fishermen were powerless to assist, as they could not launch their cobles through the breakers. The crew of thirteen were at the mercy of the storm but only five survived as they were washed ashore clinging to the wreckage of the *Adventure*.

The loss of the *Adventure* galvanised local feeling and action. The 'Gentlemen of the Lawe House', an association of South Shields shipowners, had club rooms overlooking the mouth of the Tyne and from their windows they witnessed many wrecks including the ill-fated *Adventure*. A sailor's life was considered cheap in those days, sometimes rarely getting a mention in a local newspaper, but the loss of a vessel was a highly visible and expensive event for a shipowner. They determined that something must be done and offered a prize of two guineas for ideas on how such a rescue boat – a lifeboat – could be built, which would withstand heavy damaging seas.

At about the same time William Wouldhave of Liddell Street, South Shields, a house painter and music teacher by occupation, set out to design a boat which was unsinkable and was self-righting. This was a lifeboat built for this specific purpose. Wouldhave submitted a model that was not universally accepted and he was awarded half of the prize money, one guinea. His design formed the basis of the first lifeboat, the *Original*, built by a ship's carpenter named Henry Greathead, which was launched at South Shields on the 10th June 1789. So the work started and within the next fourteen years thirty boats were built as lifeboats at South Shields.

It was now imperative to establish a lifeboat service for the whole country and in 1824 the Royal National Lifeboat Institution was founded.

The lifeboat *Original* from a contemporary print.

Many of the lifeboat stations around the country have families that claim a long association with service to the lifeboat, none more so than Cullercoats. Over the generations representatives from the families of the Storeys, Smiths, Stocks, Olivers, Lisles, Bruntons and Taylors have given unstinting and unremitting service.

The women of the village have more than played their part also. They were always among the first to help at a launch in the days before tractors, risking injury to get the boat away, and they worked tirelessly behind the scenes collecting money for the lifeboat cause.

Cullercoats Lifeboat Station celebrated its 150th anniversary in July 2002. The crews of the Cullercoats lifeboats were drawn, by and large, from the fishermen of the village and performed many of their acts of rescue for the benefit of their friends and neighbours in the fishing community. Today, with the demise of the fishing industry, the crewmembers are from all walks of life but they are no less dedicated to the RNLI. The RNLI has no motto as such, but inscribed around the medals of bravery are the words, 'Let not the deep swallow me up.'

In addition to setting up and establishing lifeboat stations around the country the RNLI also awarded medals for acts of bravery whether from lifeboat, boat or from the shore.

In 1827 Alexander Donkin was awarded a Silver Medal for the rescue of the master of the sloop *James* from the sea. A local boat manned by 9 men had attempted a rescue but they had been driven back by the ferocious seas.

Cullercoats Lifeboat Station, built 1896, where it still stands today.

A second Silver Medal was awarded to James Redford for a rescue, which took place on 26th February 1852 when, during a heavy gale, a fishing boat with a crew of three foundered on the rocks as she entered the bay. Two men were drowned but the third crewmember, a boy, was hauled to safety by Redford who jumped into the sea with a rope and swam to the boy's assistance.

Andrew (Dolly) Taylor was the third recipient to be awarded a Silver Medal. In 1898 he retired as coxswain of the lifeboat due to ill health after almost 30 years service as coxswain. As a mark of respect to his dedicated service he was award a Silver Medal.

During the time that the big lifeboats were stationed at Cullercoats there were only ten coxswains of these boats. They deserve recognition for their dedication and as a mark of respect they are detailed here.

Name of Coxswain	Length of Service
John Redford	1852-69
Andrew (Dolly) Taylor	1869-98
George Lisle	1898-1920
Joseph Taylor	1920-23
James Scott	1923-29
Robert Arthur	1929-33
George Brunton	1933-39
James Taylor	1939-57
George Scott Taylor	1957-63
Raymond Oliver	1963-69

Andrew 'Dolly' Taylor, recipient of a Silver Award for meritorious service, coxswain from 1869-98.

In 1848 a coble manned by seven local men was taking a pilot to a ship bound for South Shields when it capsized, with the loss of all aboard. The account of this disaster is chronicled elsewhere in this book. The disaster greatly upset the Duke of Northumberland, who owned much of the land around Cullercoats, and he provided funds so that the RNLI could establish a lifeboat station at Cullercoats.

In 1852 a lifeboat and its launching carriage were delivered to Cullercoats. The lifeboat, named *Percy*, was powered by 10 oars, was 30 feet long by 8 feet wide, and had been built at the Duke's expense. The

Percy had been built of elm in the Royal Naval Dockyards at Woolwich. She was soon to be used and saw regular service escorting the local fleet of cobles when they were in danger from bad weather, as well as performing rescues on larger ships which came to grief on the local coast. In 1859, the *Percy* was found to be suffering from dry rot and was condemned. In her life she had been launched 7 times and was credited with saving 9 lives.

She was replaced with a slightly larger boat, again built at the Duke of Northumberland's expense and again called *Percy*. The lifeboat cost £174. This boat performed a famous rescue in 1861 when, because of bad weather which prevented her being launched at Cullercoats, she was dragged several miles along the coast to Whitley Bay to go to the rescue of the crew of the brig *Lovely Nelly*. In her life she had been launched 6 times and was credited with saving 15 lives.

In 1866 the *Percy* was replaced with a lifeboat donated by Mr Peter Reid of the London Stock Exchange. The lifeboat cost £275. The *Percy* was refitted and transferred to Fraserburgh and renamed *Havelock*. The new lifeboat, *Palmerston*, was also built to a 10-oar design and served at Cullercoats until 1884. During her career at Cullercoats, *Palmerston* was credited with saving 65 lives. Her most famous rescue was the saving of 21 crew and 8 passengers from the steamship *Libelle*.

The author's son, Christopher Wright, a proud crewmember on Cullercoats lifeboat for many years. Contrast his survival equipment with that of Andrew 'Dolly' Taylor.

The provision of lifeboats has always been due to the generosity of individuals and the collective donations from members of the public but in 1884, an act of corporate generosity by the Co-operative Wholesale Society presented Cullercoats RNLI with her fourth new lifeboat. The lifeboat was built to celebrate the Society's 25th anniversary, cost £385 and was appropriately called *Co-operator No 1*. Built by the established firm of Forrests of Limehouse, the lifeboat was built of mahogany and combined all of the latest improvements in self-righting. Thirty-seven feet long with a beam of 8 feet she was now able to carry an additional set of oars making 12 in all. She served the lifeboat station well with uninterrupted continuous service at Cullercoats until 1907. She was broken up the following year.

George Lisle, coxswain 1898-1920. He retired as coxswain at the age of 77 years.

In 1896 the present boathouse was built and once again paid for by the Co-operative Wholesale Society. The building has continued to provide a safe haven for the lifeboat and its crews for over a hundred years. The lifeboat station is open to members of the public and there is a small photographic museum on the walls of the station.

The Co-operative Wholesale Society's generosity was demonstrated again in 1907, when it funded the next replacement at Cullercoats, also called *Co-operator No 1* at a cost of £879. This new boat was to remain in service until 1937 during which time it was credited with rescuing 102 people.

Up until 1937 all the lifeboats at Cullercoats had been 'Pulling and Sailing' types, which were propelled by oars and, when suitable, sails.

Once they were in the area of the rescue, they used the lifeboat's oars, which gave them greater control over the boat. The march of progress changed this in 1937, when the first motor lifeboat was placed on station at Cullercoats. She was the single-engined *Richard Silver Oliver*, which also had sails for use in the event of engine failure.

The *Richard Silver Oliver* had a short and tragic career at Cullercoats. During an exercise on 22nd April 1939, the lifeboat was overwhelmed by a freak wave off Tynemouth and six of the ten people aboard were drowned. Although the lifeboat suffered only superficial damage and a replacement crew was quickly found for the crewmembers that had lost their lives, the *Richard Silver Oliver* was withdrawn from service at Cullercoats. She went on to serve at Newquay, Ilfracombe and Criccieth and left the service in 1963.

George Scott Taylor, coxswain 1957-63.

Cullercoats lifeboat station retuned to full active service in February 1940 with the lifeboat *Westmorland* that had previously served at Berwick. The *Westmorland* was 35.5 feet long and had cost £4,597. She saw service until 1951 and was credited with saving 101 lives, 95 of them during the Second World War.

The next lifeboat at Cullercoats was the *Isaac and Mary Bolton*, a twin-engined self-righting boat with a speed of 7$\frac{1}{2}$ knots. By now this replacement had cost £12,548 and had been provided from a legacy of Miss Mary Bolton of Bootle and a gift of the Lord Lieutenant of Northumberland's War Distress Relief Fund. The *Isaac and Mary Bolton* continued in service for 12 years until 1963 and was credited with saving 31 lives.

In November of 1963, a new lifeboat, *Sir James Knott*, an Oakley class boat with a top speed of $8^1/_2$ knots was stationed at Cullercoats. Again, the boat had largely been provided by generous donations from a private individual, this time one with local connections. The lifeboat cost £33,000 and was provided mainly from the funds of the Sir James Knott Trust. In her life she had been launched 29 times and was credited with saving 31 lives.

Raymond Oliver, coxswain 1963-69.

At about the same time, the RNLI introduced the first of the inflatable rescue boats, stationing one at Cullercoats in 1965. These boats only required a crew of two or three and used a succession of fast, inflatable lifeboats, known as D and C Class boats. It was considered at this time that the incidents occurring around Cullercoats were requiring the services of the inshore boat and as a result of an RNLI review, it was decided to stand the Cullercoats station down from year-round duty. In 1969 the *Sir James Knott* was assigned elsewhere, having saved 14 lives during her stay at Cullercoats. One hundred and seventeen years of full service appeared to have come to an end. In that period the big lifeboats at Cullercoats Lifeboat Station were credited with saving 351 lives.

In April 2002 it was calculated that in its history, the lifeboats of Cullercoats had been launched 684 times and were credited with saving 570 lives.

Lifeboats through the Ages

The first *Co-operator No 1* with the coxswain Andrew 'Dolly' Taylor by the carriage wheel on the left.

Lifeboat *Co-operator No 1*, *circa* 1900.

The second of the lifeboats to be called *Co-operator No 1*.

The last of the big lifeboats stationed at Cullercoats, the *Sir James Knott*.

The fishermen of Cullercoats were highly respected seamen and apart from performing unstinting service with the Cullercoats lifeboat, many local men also served on the Tynemouth lifeboat.

One of the most famous was Robert 'Scraper' Smith who lived in Garden Square, Cullercoats. Born in 1856 into a fishing family he knew nothing else and by the age of 12 years, in keeping with his contemporaries, he was a crewmember of a local fishing boat.

'Scraper' Smith was a modest man, a teetotaller and non-smoker. He was also a devout man and a staunch supporter and choir member of the local Methodist Church. Such was his commitment to his church and religion it is reported that he only missed three Christmas services in a fifty-year period. Like many Cullercoats fishermen he had a large family of six sons and three daughters, although, two sons and one daughter died before they reached adulthood.

Like many of his ilk Smith was greatly affected by the wreck of the *Stanley* in 1864 on the Black Midden Rocks at North Shields, which claimed the lives of twenty-four people despite heroic but unsuccessful attempts of rescue from the shore. Their cries of help, which he could not answer, remained with him for many years and as soon as he was able to pull on an oar he joined the volunteer lifeboat service.

Robert Smith was 54 years of age when he was appointed the coxswain of the Tynemouth lifeboat *J McConnell Hussey*, a pulling/sailing lifeboat which had been converted to motor power. Within a year she was replaced with Tynemouth's first purpose-built motor lifeboat, the *Henry Vernon*, which had been provided through a legacy from Mrs Arabella Vernon, of Weston-upon-Mare. The *Henry Vernon* and Robert 'Scraper' Smith were destined to become renowned for their part in the rescue of the crew and passengers of HM Hospital Ship *Rohilla*. This rescue confirmed the value of motor propulsion for lifeboats and the rescue captured the imagination of a nation at war.

The *Rohilla* was a 7,000-ton ship, which set out for Dunkirk on 30th October 1914 in the third month of the First World War, with a complement of 229 crew and medical staff. Her task was to collect wounded soldiers in urgent need of medical treatment. As it was wartime there were no lights on the coast of Britain and the *Rohilla* was travelling in darkness. Navigation was by the light of the moon and the stars. The *Rohilla* was steaming into a gale when she drove ashore on the Saltwick Nab Rocks, three quarters of a mile outside of Whitby Harbour. Tremendous seas started washing over her and some of the crew took to the rigging seeking safety.

Four lifeboats including one summoned from the Tees attempted to reach the ship but were beaten back by the ferocity of the seas. The Whitby No 1 lifeboat, *Robert and Mary Ellis*, could not leave Whitby Harbour because of the ferocious seas. The Whitby No 2 lifeboat, *John Fielden*, had to be manhandled over an eight-foot seawall in order to launch it and another lifeboat from Upgang, north of Whitby, *William Riley of Birmingham and Leamington*, had to be lowered hundreds of feet down the cliffs. The Whitby lifeboat, *John Fielden*, did manage to affect two rescues collecting 41 people but was severely damaged in the attempt and could not continue with any further rescue attempts. These lifeboats were not motor powered but pulling and sailing lifeboats. Other lifeboats from Scarborough, the *Queensbury*, and Redcar, *Fifi and Charles*, tried to render assistance but could not get to the ship because of the tremendous seas.

The rescue went on for 36 hours as the *Rohilla* lay there gradually breaking up in the seas. Some of the ship's complement, having given up any chance of rescue, attempted to swim to the shore. Sixty people made it but many perished in the cold angry seas.

The nearest motor lifeboat to the scene of the disaster was the Tynemouth-based *Henry Vernon*. A telegram message was sent to the Tynemouth Station requesting help and the *Henry Vernon* set sail in atrocious weather to render assistance. The telegram simply stated, 'Please despatch motor lifeboat to wreck of *Rohilla* at Saltwick, Whitby. About 40 persons remaining on board. Ordinary lifeboats have failed to reach her.'

The hospital ship *Rohilla* off Whitby Sands.

Robert 'Scraper' Smith was the coxswain. The lifeboat took all night to travel the 45 nautical miles to Whitby and upon arrival she docked at Whitby harbour to replenish her fuel oil and await daybreak. The weather had not abated and the *Rohilla* was lying broadside on towards the raging seas that were breaking right over the stricken vessel. The *Henry Vernon* approached the *Rohilla* from the seaward side, something the pulling lifeboats could not have done, and discharged oil into the seas to calm them. She then raced shoreward through the surf, turned broadside to the waves and came in under the leeward side of the *Rohilla* and ran in close alongside. Despite being submerged by the seas breaking over the *Rohilla* the lifeboat managed to rescue the remaining fifty-one people left on board the ship. The last to leave the ship was Captain Neilson who inquired before leaving the ship if everyone had been saved. 'All but one, sir,' one of the crew shouted from the lifeboat; 'I've left my kitten.' Neilson went back into the wheelhouse and emerged with the kitten. Their ordeal had lasted for fifty-nine hours.

However, the lifeboat's ordeal was not over. As she left the shelter of the *Rohilla* she was hit broadside on by two enormous waves that knocked her on her beam-ends and she disappeared into the foam and spray shortly to rise clear and escape into the refuge of the harbour.

This rescue over two days and nights remains one of the great achievements of the RNLI. One hundred and forty-eight people survived the ordeal but eight-four perished. The boat superintendent, Major H.E. Burton, and the coxswain, Robert 'Scraper' Smith, was awarded the highest honour that the RNLI could bestow, the Gold Medal for conspicuous bravery, the nautical equivalent of the Victoria Cross. The second coxswain of the lifeboat, James S. Brownlee, was awarded a Silver Medal.

The Gold Medal for bravery was not the first or the last medal for bravery that Robert Smith received. On 11th January 1913 the steamship *Dunelm* of Sunderland was stranded and wrecked during a heavy gale and huge seas off the South Pier at Blyth. The Blyth lifeboat could not affect a rescue and requested assistance from the Tynemouth motor lifeboat *Henry Vernon*. Robert Smith, as coxswain, with a reduced crew of five immediately launched the Tynemouth lifeboat and rendered assistance arriving at the wreck one and half hours later and just as the last member of the crew was rescued by breeches buoy. The lifeboat immediately set course to return to Tynemouth but on the return journey Smith was badly hurt when he was thrown against the stern of the lifeboat by the heavy seas fracturing his ribs. It was reported that no one in living memory could remember the seas being in such a menacing state and as a result of this rescue Robert Smith was awarded a Silver Medal for bravery.

Robert 'Scraper' Smith completed his hat-trick when he was awarded another Silver Medal following the rescue of the crew from the steamship *Muristan* of Swansea. On 20th November 1916 the *Muristan* ran ashore in Blyth Bay after her steering gear failed and immediately began to break up. The Blyth sailing and pulling lifeboat was powerless to assist, due to the prevailing weather conditions and the closeness to shore of the *Muristan,* so a request was made to the Tynemouth lifeboat to render assistance.

The *Henry Vernon* struggled to the scene but had to shelter in Blyth Harbour until an opportune moment came to attempt a rescue. By now only the bridge and the charthouse were visible over the huge waves and the area was strewn with wreckage. Smith took the lifeboat as close as he could but could see no signs of life. He decided to return to Tynemouth but as he started to head for home the *Henry Vernon* was hit by a huge wave and the engine disabled. The *Henry Vernon* resorted to sail power and successfully navigated itself into Blyth Harbour.

Over the next twenty-four hours the engine of the *Henry Vernon* was stripped down and rebuilt and as the weather conditions improved the local coastguard reported seeing signs of life on board the *Muristan*. The lifeboat immediately rendered assistance and was surprised and amazed to find the sixteen crew members still alive and huddled together in the chart room. They were successfully rescued and landed at Blyth Harbour to the delight of the local population.

Robert 'Scraper' Smith retired in 1920, whilst still in good health, although his sight was beginning to fail. In 1924 he was to receive his highest award in recognition for his gallantry. Accompanied by his daughter Hilda he travelled to Buckingham Palace to receive the Empire Gallantry Medal from King George V. What should have been a joyous event was tinged by sadness when 'Scraper' Smith, due to his poor eyesight, failed to realise that he had been presented to the King as he was expecting him to be dressed in his naval uniform. The King chose on the day to wear civilian clothing. It was not until he asked a fellow lifeboat man when they would meet his Majesty that he was told, 'You've just been talking to him Scraper.' The moment that he had been waiting for so long had gone to his great disappointment.

The whole of Cullercoats village was immensely proud of his achievements and upon his return to the village he was astounded to find crowds lining the street as he walked to his home in Garden Square. Once home the well-wishers gave him a rousing chorus of 'for he's a jolly good fellow.'

Annie Dodds, Mary Ellen Scott, Robert 'Scraper' Smith, Hilda Smith (daughter) and Lizzie Proudfoot.

On 30th October 1927, at the age of 78 years, 'Scraper' Smith died, almost thirteen years to the day of the *Rohilla* rescue. By now he was totally blind and no longer able to see Cullercoats Bay and his little red, white and white coble. His hearing, however, was still acute and he went to his final resting place listening to the waves pounding on the rocks beneath his house.

'Scraper' Smith disliked publicity and would never have seen himself as a hero but there is no doubt that he was and the village of Cullercoats can be rightly proud of him. In this day of instant fame and gratification the term hero is used to describe footballers, celebrities and many people less deserving than Robert 'Scraper' Smith.

Although not a Cullercoats fisherman or Cullercoats lifeboat man, this picture of the coxswain of Tynemouth lifeboat, James Gilbert, gives a detailed indication of what rudimentary equipment that these brave man had when they went to sea to unselfishly rescue others in peril. 'Scraper' Smith's favourite saying, 'You can't play with the sea,' are wise words.

CLIFF HOUSE

Cliff House, 2002.

In 1768 Captain Thomas Armstrong, a Customs Officer, built Bank Top House which later became known as Cliff House. His eighteenth century Georgian house has a stunning aspect with open views out to sea both to the north and particularly to the south. Featured in the BBC documentary programme *House Detectives*, the house is the subject of many legends.

Thomas Armstrong, of North Shields, was the commander of His Majesty's Cutter, *Bridlington*, a customs vessel used to patrol the seas from Newcastle to Sunderland, with a remit to intercept smugglers. He was ruthless and ambitious. Armstrong was obviously wealthy, as he could afford to purchase a plot of land at Cullercoats to build a house. Yet his riches were a puzzle, as the pay attached to his post, was not commensurate with the ability to build Cliff House

Amongst the most interesting features of the house is that it had a huge underground cellar, with wrought iron bars separating prison type cells. Smuggling was a basic Cullercoats industry by this time. By 1771 the cellar was being used to store contraband goods but it was also reputed to have been a stronghold for the contrabandists themselves. In 1771 Armstrong was charged and convicted of permitting smugglers to escape and giving false accounts of goods that he had allegedly seized. He was suspended for 3 months and fined.

Cliff House, Bank Top and Back Row. A secret tunnel ran from Cliff House on to the beach below.

Armstrong's dubious character continued and it is clear by the mid 1770s that Thomas Armstrong and his family were feared in the locality, using the local constables at will and acting as though they were above the law. The final straw came in 1776, when Thomas and his associates deliberately allowed two notorious smugglers to escape from their care. Thomas and his officers had prevented the crew from locking the smugglers in the ship's brig, allowing them to roam free on deck. Indeed they were upon such goods terms with the smugglers that they frequently dined and drank wine and beer together. In this case the two smugglers seem to have been able to simply jump into a boat leisurely rowing themselves to safety and freedom. Armstrong was dismissed from the service.

His secret life of crime can still be seen in Cliff House and helps to explain some of the unique architectural features of his house – iron cages in the cellar and a secret passage accessed by a trapdoor in his study, which was found by the House Detectives. In the 1960s the sea defence walls were built outside of Cliff House and during this construction they discovered a secret passage dug into the cliff, which led from Cliff House down through the cliff on to the small beach below the house. Unfortunately this find was not adequately researched and recorded before the sea wall once again hid this secret passageway. Goods could therefore be delivered and stored unnoticed by all and it is clear that much of Armstrong's wealth had come via this protection racket with the smugglers.

The Armstrong family retained ownership of the house until 1837 when it was sold to Harry Hewitson. An adjoining cottage to Cliff House built in 1720 was merged with Cliff House, together with another cottage in 1840 and the house now represents the sum of three properties.

Robert Arkwright was the son of Sir Richard Arkwright, the inventor of the spinning frame. In 1846 he bought Cliff House for the benefit of his wife Fanny, the daughter of a theatrical manager and actor well known in the North of England. Mrs Arkwright was celebrated both for her beauty and accomplishments and for her family connections with the stage. Her cousin Frances Ann Kemble referred to the residence in her journal *Record of a Girlhood*:

'The loss of her favourite son affected her with irrecoverable sorrow, and she passed a great portion of the last years of her life in a place called Cullercoats, a little fishing village on the north coast, to which, when a young girl she used to accompany her father and mother for rest and refreshment, when the hard life from which her marriage released her allowed them a few days respite by the rocks and sands and breakers of the Northumbrian Shore. The Duke of Devonshire whose infirmity of deafness did not interfere with his enjoyment of music was an enthusiastic admirer of Mrs Arkwright and her constant and affectionate friend. Their proximity of residence in Derbyshire made their opportunities for meeting very frequent and when the Arkwrights visited London, Devonshire House, was if they chose their hotel. His attachment to her induced him towards the end of his life to take a residence in the poor little village of Cullercoats whither she loved to resort and where she died.'

The celebrated beauty of Mrs Arkwright captured in a drawing commissioned by the Duke of Devonshire.

I allow the reader to interpret the above passage but it is believed that the Duke of Devonshire had little interest in women although it is clear that he was besotted with the beauty of Fanny Kemble.

This romantic theme between Fanny and the Duke of Devonshire is reflected in the Duke's bedroom at Cliff House, which is similar to bedrooms at the Duke of Devonshire's ancestral home at Chatsworth in Derbyshire.

The house has changed hands many times over the years but since 1998 the house has resumed it traditional links with the stage when Rosalind Bailey, a well-known local actress, purchased the property. Mrs Bailey has always loved the house and realised her dream of owning the property. It is to her credit that the house has been restored to such a high standard.

THE LEGACY OF AN AMERICAN IN CULLERCOATS

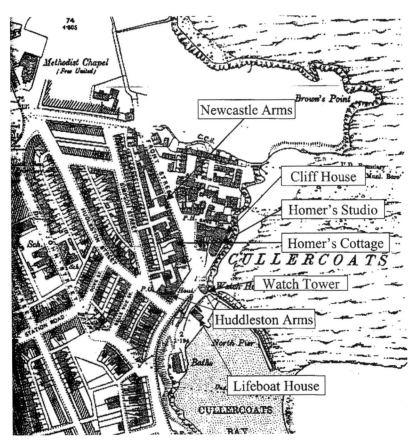

Plan of Cullercoats showing the location of the various addresses described in this section.

Tyneside two centuries ago produced a succession of artists who spent most or all of their lives in the North East and painted almost exclusively the landscapes and people of the area. The character and uniqueness of Cullercoats captured the imagination of artists and remains today one of the most painted localities in Northumberland.

Thomas Richardson and John Wilson Carmichael both painted here in the 1820s and Robert Jobling settled in the area. Robert Jobling's major Cullercoats work hangs in the Laing Art Gallery, Newcastle. Its title 'The day is done and darkness falls from the wings of night' depicts Cullercoats fishwives making for home along the beach beneath the Watch Tower as dusk approaches. It is a fine painting but is not representative of actuality. Fish were always landed by the time of this painting in the early morning but this error of fact does not distract for its mood and beauty.

However, the most famous of all the painters to capture Cullercoats on canvas was the American watercolour artist Winslow Homer who arrived in 1881.

Winslow Homer shortly after his return to the USA.

Winslow Homer is for many people America's greatest artist. How the artist in the early part of 1881 came to Cullercoats has been the subject of much debate. He apparently arrived as a stranger from across the seas whose unheralded presence in the clannish and insular village must have excited the curiosity of the village.

Few of the inhabitants of the village had ventured much further than 10 miles away from their homes and a stranger from a country, many of whom would never of heard of, surely fascinated them.

It has been suggested that it was a mere accident that Homer chose the village of Cullercoats from many other better known to artists of that time, but perhaps there is a more logical reason.

Winslow Homer was born in Boston, Massachusetts, USA in February 1856 and by the mid 1870s he was regarded as an accomplished artist. In the spring of 1881 he made his second voyage abroad to Europe when he sailed from New York to Liverpool aboard the Cunard liner SS *Parthia*. It is believed that he intended to make Scarborough his final destination. As an artist he may have heard of the popularity of Cullercoats and it is believed that he had a friend in New York who had spent his childhood in Newcastle.

Tony Harrison in his excellent publication, *Winslow Homer in Cullercoats*, has researched the fellow passengers on board the SS *Parthia*. Two names of interest were found. One of the passengers is listed as W. Carmichael and may have been a relative of the well-known marine, landscape, and figure artist, John William Carmichael, who was native of Newcastle. However, this passenger disembarked in Ireland before the ship reached its final destination in Liverpool, which places doubt on such a family connection.

Another passenger is listed as James Shaw. The licensee of the Queens Head public house was a man of the same name who had relatives in the United States of America. Significantly the census taken in the month of April 1881 does not list anyone resident at the public house, the entry remaining blank save for acknowledging that the pub existed. However, the SS *Parthia* docked at Liverpool on 28th March 1881 and in order for this theory to be creditable it has to be supposed that Shaw did not return home until after the date of the census.

Homer struck up a friendship with a local man of the name, Alan Blythsman Adamson, who returned to America with Homer in 1884. Adamson wrote in a memoir shortly after Homer's death: 'it was a mere accident he had chosen the village of Cullercoats from among the many others in England. On the voyage over he met a man who, when Homer mentioned his object in crossing the Atlantic told him to go to the village I had previously mentioned (Cullercoats) where he would find just the subjects for his brush that he was seeking, at the same time giving him directions as to the best way of reaching the place of his recommendation.'

However, what is certain is that Homer arrived in Cullercoats some weeks later and initially stayed in the Hudleston Arms Hotel (now the Bay Hotel). Homer rented a front room facing on to the bay but then rented a room to use as a studio at 12 Bank Top. Unfortunately this building has long ago been demolished but its location was to the south and next to Cliff House.

Homer did not remain at the Hudleston Arms for the duration of his stay and there remains some doubt as to where he took lodgings. The main body of opinion is that Homer rented a single room at 44b Front Street close to his studio.

The prolific work of Homer during his stay in the North East immortalised the beauty of the robust fisherwoman of the village who clearly fascinated him. They

A.B. Adamson in 1852 shortly before he left Cullercoats with Winslow Homer.

Winslow Homer would have had a view like this from his studio window.

were ideal subjects and were framed against a backdrop of gracefully lined cobles, moody skies and seas and foreboding clouds.

One of Homer's favourite models was Maggie Jefferson, who later married a local fisherman William Storey. She appears in a number of his works when she was aged between 12 and 13 years old. Other academics consider that she was older but the census records of 1881 clearly show her as the 12-year-old daughter of James and Isabella Jefferson and that she had two older brothers and four older sisters. The family resided at 45 Front Street, which adjoined Winslow Homer's residence.

Some of these works relate to Cullercoats paintings but he also used Maggie Jefferson on paintings depicting Flamborough Head. The interaction between these two people, who were poles apart, comes alive in these paintings and it is my belief that she appears in the following paintings but probably appears in more.

Hark the Lark
A Voice from the Cliffs
Three Girls
Four fisher girls on the beach at Tynemouth
Sketch of the Head of a Woman
Flamborough Head

43 and 44 Front Street, Cullercoats, where Homer had a lodging room.

It is also thought that the identity of a second girl on the paintings that depict three fisher girls, namely Hark the Lark, Voice from the Cliffs and Three Girls is Isabella Jefferson, who was from another Cullercoats family.

Maggie Storey lived her life restrained and confined in the village until her death in 1957 at the age of 88 years. Her husband, William Storey, had died twelve years earlier in 1945 aged 79 years. Maggie Storey bore seventeen children although not all of them survived into adulthood. At the time of writing this book, one of her children, May Thorington, is still surviving.

Pencil sketch of a fisher girl (private collection) reliably considered being that of Maggie Storey née Jefferson.

The face and beauty of Maggie Storey is known throughout the world yet she herself never ventured far from the village.

Maggie Storey, née Jefferson, Winslow Homer's favourite model.

A rare photograph of Isabella Jefferson who also sat as a model for Winslow Homer. The author is of the firm belief that the girl sitting knitting is Maggie Jefferson, later to become Maggie Storey.

WHAT MIGHT HAVE HAPPENED

Had the planners, engineers and local government got its way there would have been no grand building such as this at Tynemouth, Tynemouth Long Sands would have disappeared under concrete and Cullercoats Bay ruined for eternity.

Standing on the all-embracing granite Piers protecting the mouth of the River Tyne watching the sparse river traffic ride the 'Shields Bar' with ease as the ships head in and out of the Tyne, it is difficult to imagine how dangerous this was in the days of the sailing ships. The Piers represent to me the encirclement of a mother's arm around her baby in the way that the Piers protect the River Tyne.

In the middle years of the nineteenth century the mouth of the River Tyne was not protected by the North and South Piers – these were not completed until 1895. The Shields Bar was a constantly shifting bank of shingle, rock and sand, which formed across the mouth of the river. Safe negotiation of the bar depended on the tides, the prevailing wind conditions and the depth of the water beneath a ship's keel. Given a stiff Easterly wind the bar could become a raging maelstrom of sea, spray and foam. Many vessels foundered as they tried to enter or leave the Tyne. It was dangerous port to enter and a difficult port to leave.

The River Tyne was alive with shipping and commerce yet the river itself was suffering from years of neglect. The Tyne had become a sluggish, polluted river which was strewn with wrecks and rocks. No dredging had taken place and the sailing ships were at the mercy of Mother Nature. Yet despite these problems over 1,500 ships were registered from the Port of Tyne (which included Newcastle, North and South Shields) and sailing ships from America, Holland, Greece, France and the Baltic states were frequent visitors.

The sailing ships of the Tyne ranged from fully-rigged four-masted clipper ships to lowly coastal sloops. However, the majority of them were two and three masted barques, brigs, snows and schooners that rarely exceeded 400 registered tons. Although most of these were colliers, who plied their trade between Newcastle and London, many of them tramped around the world where their cargoes and trade took them.

Movement in and out of the Tyne was entirely dependent upon the weather. Prolonged Easterly winds prevented vessels from leaving the Tyne. In the winter of 1847-48, at the turn of the year, one thousand seven hundred vessels lay wind bound in the Tyne for several weeks. The day that the wind abated and provided favourable conditions for sailing four hundred vessels left in one tide amidst much jostling, bumping and mayhem.

Entering the Tyne in bad weather or when heavy seas were running the sailing ships made for an exciting spectacle and in such conditions many thousand of onlookers would gather on the shore. On 5th January 1841 in atrocious conditions the sloop *Newcastle and Berwick Packet* was seen running the bar for the safety of the river. The vessel disappeared in a fury of white foam as she crossed the bar but emerged unscathed, the only ship to enter the river that day. Others were less fortunate.

Leaving the harbour for the open seas was slightly less dangerous but nevertheless many vessels succumbed to disaster. Grounding the keel heavily as the vessel 'bounced' over the bar could cause severe leaks that frequently sank a vessel days later whilst on the open seas.

Fortunately many vessels left the restrictions of the Tyne safely and the local men could find themselves at the four corners of the earth provided their luck held. Many failed to reach their destination or to return home. Between 1830 and 1900 one mariner in five lost his life at sea. No other form of occupation had such an attrition rate including deep coal mining. In the same period seventy percent of all Tyne sailing ships were lost at sea as they foundered, caught fire, ran ashore, were run down by other vessels or just disappeared and were recorded as 'lost at sea.'

In 1850 it was reported to parliament that during the preceding four years 12,041 British vessels had been lost at sea. Yet there was no shortage of men ready to crew the British Merchant Fleet. In one four day period between 29th March and 1st April the Northbound fleet of colliers, which numbered five hundred, had been detained off Yarmouth due to bad weather, encountered a terrific south east gale as they reached home waters. Thirty vessels were wrecked on the Herd Sands at South Shields and on the Black Midden Rocks at North Shields, a further thirty-five were wrecked off Sunderland and seven off Hartlepool. In 1852 929 mariners lost their lives but two years later the figure had greatly increased to 1,349 lives lost with 987 ships sent to the bottom of the oceans.

Wreck of the *Farne* in October 1894 by the North Pier.

This appalling loss of life and loss of shipping caused great consternation within the country and a port of refuge at Tynemouth and Cullercoats was proposed and seriously considered. In the hope of persuading the government to give assistance for the construction of a harbour of refuge at the mouth of the Tyne, Lord Ellenborough, speaking in the House of Lords in 1854, said that, 'during January last not less than one hundred and ten ships were wrecked in the course of three days within twenty miles of the mouth of the river and thirty-six were wrecked at the mouth of the Tyne itself ... During the present year I understand that not less than fifteen hundred vessels, containing two hundred thousand tons of coal, all required for immediate use of the Metropolis, have been detained for nearly four weeks at the mouth of the Tyne, not one of them having been able to leave in consequence of the state of the bar.' While the bar foamed and seethed the inhabitants of the capital froze in their homes.

The *Waterwitch* riding the bar in safer times under towage.

An elaborate plan of massive proportions was presented, which fortunately did not come to fruition. W.A. Brooks, 26 George Street, Westminster, London, presented the plans and their size precludes their inclusion for way of illustration. However, I have faithfully replicated the plans to show the extent of their magnitude.

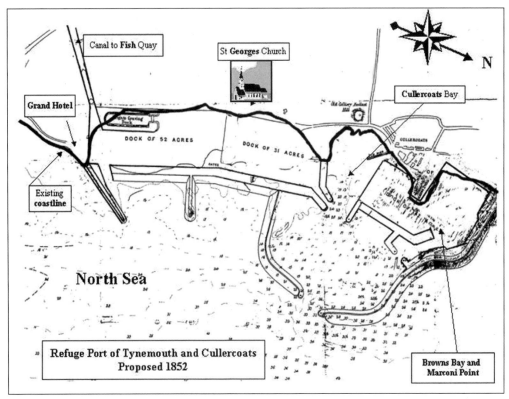

The plans for the refuge port of Tynemouth and Cullercoats proposed in 1852 and debated in the Houses of Parliament.

The plans do not need any detailed explanation as for once the plan speaks as loud as any written explanation. Suffice to say the natural beauty of the area would have been ruined with the following consequences:

Tynemouth Long Sands would have been totally obliterated and would have ceased to exist. They would have become concrete docks.

Cullercoats harbour would have been totally altered and destroyed.

Browns Bay would have disappeared under huge concrete docks.

A large dog leg Pier was to be built out from the table rocks at the north of Cullercoats with further Piers from below Cliff House, Smugglers Cave, opposite St George's Church and near to the Grand Hotel, Tynemouth.

A large concrete Pier acting as a sea defence wall would have stretched the whole length of the Tynemouth Long Sands and the area would have been permanently under water due to a sequence of lock gates.

Finally a wide canal was to be opened up from beside the Grand Hotel that would have travelled up the side of Percy Gardens to Holy Saviour's Church at Tynemouth. It would have continued past the

Dolphin public house and past the Golf Course and into Northumberland Park before it exited into the river at Clifford's Fort by the North Shields Fish Quay.

The purpose of this grandiose scheme was to be able regulate the traffic in and out of the River Tyne which was no longer dependent upon the vagrancies of the weather.

The march of progress is fickle, inconsistent and erratic. History has fortunately shown that this scheme failed. Had it not done so the area would have been irreparably ruined for generations. There would today have been no Tynemouth Long Sands, no picturesque Cullercoats Bay and Village and there would have been no paintings by Winslow Homer.

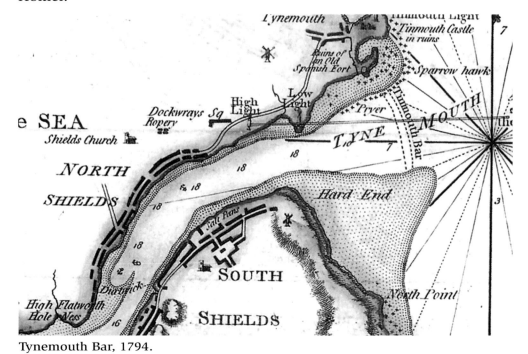

Tynemouth Bar, 1794.

The People's History

To receive a catalogue of our latest titles send a large SAE to:

The People's History
Suite 1, Byron House
Seaham Grange Business Park
Seaham, County Durham
SR7 0PY

www.thepeopleshistory.co.uk